Inspiring Learning Through Cooking

Cooking provides children with a wealth of opportunities to discover new materials and processes; develop their physical and social skills; and lead their own learning. Helping teachers and practitioners make the most of the valuable learning opportunities that cooking offers, this book provides all the information, support and inspiration needed to successfully introduce cooking into Early Years and Key Stage One provision.

Packed with practical tips, case studies and first-hand advice from teachers and practitioners, *Inspiring Learning Through Cooking* offers valuable guidance on everything from setting up a cooking area to growing your own produce and using cooking activities to the full benefit of the child. With over 600 colour images and 50 step-by-step, photocopiable recipes, suggested cooking activities are suitable for independent use by children. Recipes reflect and promote the ongoing development of children's skills, and illustrate how cooking can be used to achieve learning objectives. Teachers and practitioners will be inspired to think creatively about their own provision, and promote open-ended learning, encourage decision-making, problem solving and collaboration through cooking.

Colourful, practical and accessible, *Inspiring Learning Through Cooking* will be an essential resource for Early Years' practitioners and teachers looking to explore the opportunities offered by cooking in nurseries, Reception, Years One and Two.

Suzie Strutt has taught in Early Years and Key Stage One for 14 years and is an experienced Early Years and Key Stage One Team Leader.

Inspiring Learning Through Cooking

Suzie Strutt

Routledge
Taylor & Francis Group

LONDON AND NEW YORK

First published 2019
by Routledge
2 Park Square, Milton Park, Abingdon, Oxon OX14 4RN

and by Routledge
52 Vanderbilt Avenue, New York, NY 10017

Routledge is an imprint of the Taylor & Francis Group, an informa business

© 2019 Suzie Strutt

British Library Cataloguing-in-Publication Data
A catalogue record for this book is available from the British Library

Library of Congress Cataloging-in-Publication Data
Names: Strutt, Suzie, author.
Title: Inspiring learning Through cooking / Suzie Strutt.
Description: Abingdon, Oxon ; New York, NY : Routledge, 2019. |
    Includes index.
Identifiers: LCCN 2018046779 | ISBN 9781138485662 (hb : alk. paper) |
    ISBN 9781138485679 (pb : alk. paper)
Subjects: LCSH: Early childhood education—Activity programs |
    Cooking—Study and teaching (Early childhood)—Activity programs.
Classification: LCC LB1139.35.A37 S76 2019 | DDC 372.21—dc23
LC record available at https://lccn.loc.gov/2018046779

ISBN: 978-1-138-48566-2 (hbk)
ISBN: 978-1-138-48567-9 (pbk)
ISBN: 978-1-351-04848-4 (ebk)

Typeset in Univers
by Apex CoVantage, LLC

Thank you to all the schools, pre-schools and nursery schools that are involved in this book for embracing cooking with such enthusiasm and ambition. Without your hard work and dedication this book would not have been possible.

Thank you to my lovely husband Nick, for the countless trips to the supermarket and to my own two little chefs, Jack and Lauren, for making me smile every day.
A special thanks to Stacey, forever my job share!

Contents

Acknowledgements

I would like to thank all the Schools, Pre-Schools and Nurseries involved in this book. They were so enthusiastic about setting up their cooking and snack areas, trying the recipes and fully immersing themselves in the project.

Their journeys have formed the advice, tips and recipes in the book and without them it would not have been possible. It has truly been a pleasure working with each unique setting and watching their children enjoy and learn from cooking.

St Peter's Catholic Primary School, Surrey, UK
St Michael's Church of England (VA) Primary School, Hertfordshire, UK
Thorley Hill Primary School, Hertfordshire, UK
Trekenner Community Primary School, Cornwall, UK
Ashleigh Church of England (VC) Primary School, Devon, UK
Decoy Community Primary School, Devon, UK
Norton Pre-School, Worcester, UK
St Giles Nursery School, Lincolnshire, UK
St Mary's Broughton Gifford Primary School, Wiltshire, UK
Sunflowers Pre-School, Hertfordshire, UK

I would like to especially thank Stacey Hynd, Kelli Stocker, Holly Skinner and Victoria Farrelly for leading the projects at their schools and giving me so much of their time and energy. They are all amazing teachers who have each inspired me in their own way.

I would also like to thank Anna Ephgrave for inspiring me and giving me the confidence to teach in a way I love – a wonderful gift which I will always appreciate.

Thank you to Elsbeth Wright and Annamarie Kino at Routledge for all the advice and support along the way and for helping to make an idea a reality.

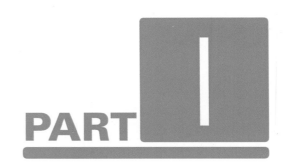

PART 1

Cooking as a tool
for learning

CHAPTER 1

Introduction

My journey

When working as Early Years and Year One Leader, I introduced cooking as a tool for learning after reading Anna Ephgrave's book *The Reception Year in Action* and teaching children how to make a cake independently. As soon as I introduced a cooking area into our learning environment you could see the engagement and learning opportunities it enabled. Cooking is so empowering for children, giving them the ability to work from start to finish to make something real and purposeful.

Wanting to build upon this learning, I started to create further opportunities in the cooking area, adding recipes for biscuits and bread. Creating a few simple recipes for children to follow independently, I soon realised the potential that independence within cooking creates. Providing a few simple recipes and introducing them to basic equipment and ingredients meant that children could follow instructions at a level which was suitable for them and achieve amazing results.

These basic recipes gave us a good starting point and as our confidence as a team grew, we encouraged the children to take more control in this area, to use their own ideas for recipes, bring in recipes from home and write their own. They began to move freely between provided recipes and each child began to produce unique products, even when they had followed the same recipe as their peers. Our cooking area became like any other of provision, where the children were in control of their own learning.

We also upgraded the snack area, adding chopping boards, knives, plates and bowls for children to prepare their own snacks. As we became more confident, we added simple recipe cards for the children to follow whilst they were preparing a snack. This changed the overall feel of the snack area as it enabled children to work on their physical skills, think carefully about the food they were preparing and explore combinations of tastes and textures, independently creating snacks they were proud of and excited to eat.

As a school we made the decision to introduce more continuous provision into Key Stage One and added a cooking area into Year One. We began making recipes for Key Stage One to reflect the next level of challenge. I strongly believe that children learn best when are given time to lead their own learning, follow their interests and work in collaboration with their peers. It is essential that as teachers we provide a rich learning environment where the children can access high quality learning experiences. In Key Stage One we need to give children time to apply the skills and concepts they have learnt in purposeful contexts to ensure they have the time to fully embed learning. Cooking is the perfect place for this as it is such an engaging area where children are eager to be involved.

When I observed children using the cooking areas I witnessed a high level of engagement and involvement. This level of engagement and involvement is crucial to children's learning.

"When children are displaying deep levels of involvement there is increased brain activity and synapse formation (i.e. learning)."

Anna Ephgrave, *Planning in the Moment with Young Children*, Routledge, Oxon, 2018

The children seemed to relish the responsibility they were given when cooking, and they loved the 'realness' of the experience, often staying on task for sustained periods of time and being fully involved in every aspect of the process.

The pleasure and pride shown by children when they had created something themselves was enchanting and cooking was soon a very popular area in both Reception and Year One.

The cooking project

Seeing children so heavily engaged and learning so much from the introduction of one area of learning gave me a small indication of the impact that cooking provision could have, and I decided I wanted to inspire other schools to introduce cooking into daily provision so that many children could benefit from the same rich learning opportunity.

In 2017/18 I embarked on a cooking project working with a variety of settings/schools who each introduced cooking areas into their provision. The settings included Pre-Schools, Nurseries and Schools. Each setting approached the project in a way which suited their own ethos and style of teaching and learning. Teachers, members of SLT, support staff and parents have all been involved in feeding back on the provision and recipes and throughout the project I observed the impact of introducing the provision, picking up practical tips and advice from teachers and staff working within each setting.

I created recipes for the settings to use from Nursery to Year Two. The recipes were designed to increase in challenge through the year groups, so they require different skills and match the challenge needed for different children. Each cohort is different so I encouraged teachers to select recipes based on the needs, interests and experiences of their own class rather than use a recipe because it was meant to be in a specific year group.

The recipes were there as a starting point, but it was up to teachers and practitioners how they were used. I encouraged teachers to keep them as open-ended as possible. Many of the recipes are designed to encourage children to be exploratory.

Throughout the project, the more the children were encouraged to experiment and design their own products, the more successful the area became. This might have been making their own unique smoothie, choosing their own pizza topping or writing their own recipe and following it. Once the basics for cooking had been established and the adults felt comfortable letting the children take control in the area, the children soon realised they could be inventive and initiate their own learning. They created their own products, adapted ones they had made before and thought of their own. Once the children become confident in this area the possibilities are endless and the project showed this time and time again.

"The children took ownership and wanted to test out their ideas for making cakes – what happens if we put hot chocolate in the cake? What happens if we put red and green food dye in? They would make predictions and discover if they were right or wrong. I think they adapted every recipe in some way after they were confident enough to follow the instructions."

Hayley Simmons, EYFS lead, St Peter's Catholic Primary School

The area is designed to be used a resource for learning. There have been many instances of children in the case studies using the cooking area, just like any other area of learning, to follow their own interests. Skilled adults have been able to use these interests and the cooking area to create wonderful learning opportunities. Here is an example of how the cooking area was used as a resource during child-initiated learning.

During the week of the royal wedding the children decided to hold a banquet in the mud kitchen. This led to discussions about the Royal Wedding and we began to find out more information together. As I had recently got married we used this as a tool to look at the components of a wedding and the different roles and things that may need to be prepared. Someone suggested that they would need a wedding cake for the royal wedding. We looked at pictures of different wedding cakes and also my cake as the children had eaten lots of it in the snack shack. We looked at the different tiers and discussed the sizes and shapes.

The children were already used to baking circular cakes as it is an option in the cooking area. As part of our discussion two children were looking at how many eggs we would need to collect from the chickens. We talked about how the bottom cake would need the most ingredients, then the middle cake and finally the top would need the least as it was the smallest. Using their understanding of the method of using the scales to balance the ingredients, the girls decided that the bottom cake would need four eggs, the middle three and the top two, drawing on previous knowledge that one egg made a flat round cake. We sourced different sized tins and ensured that they could be stacked on top of each other to look the way we wanted.

The girls made their cakes independently; before they went into the oven we talked about cooking timings. With some support the girls came to the conclusion the biggest cake would take the longest to cook, and we investigated this during cooking, reporting back to the class their findings.

After the cakes had been baked and cooled a small group of children with a gross motor focus began rolling the icing, using the techniques we had learnt when we made our jam tarts. Finally they were ready to be assembled and iced. During this time, some of the children decided to hold their own royal wedding and had been busy practicing being the Priest, dancing and making their own wedding dress. We decided to hold a royal wedding and the cake was brought out before the first dance to be cut and shared among everyone. It was delicious.

During the making of the royal wedding cake we were inundated with learning opportunities. There was so much rich mathematical language happening, children were comparing sizes, estimating, checking and recording results. The children worked together and took ownership over a project from the start to finish, checking on the different stages and thinking about next steps. They loved having an end project that could be used within their play too. It led to different writing opportunities and since making it we have explored 'bigger cakes' further even looking at how we could equally distribute a cake between 30.

Hayley Simmons, EYFS lead, St Peter's Catholic Primary School

The benefits of cooking

The Schools, Pre-Schools and Nurseries involved in the project noticed many benefits from introducing cooking into their provision. One of the biggest benefits was the impact on communication and language as well as personal and social skills. This could be seen in all cases, from where the snack area had been up levelled in Pre-Schools to making scones as a group in Year Two.

The need for children to communicate and work together effectively comes not only from their desire to do so but because the success of the product depends on it. The Early Years Foundation Stage (EYFS) recipes are an introduction to this, with the children creating their own products but sharing ingredients and equipment.

As the recipes became more of challenge, the negotiation skills became more complex. The children had to give out roles, decide who would do what and for how long. The children became more skilled in this the more they had the chance to work in this way. During the project, I listened to children negotiate/debate and reach consensus and for me, this is one of the most powerful aspects of the provision. They have to communicate, reach shared expectations, regulate their own group and decide what is acceptable and what is not.

As adults it is easy to step in and set rules for sharing but it is of far more value to allow children the opportunity to do this. They will often spend a long time debating and if left to, they will often work out a fair outcome which pleases all.

Without successful negotiation and communication, the end product may not be successful, and the children soon realised that working as a team was therefore essential. Development Matters (2012) suggests that our environment provides opportunities that require give and take and this is so evident in this area of provision.

Sometimes when mistakes were made which affected the product e.g. using salt instead of sugar or using tablespoons instead of teaspoons, teachers discovered one of the children knew what had gone wrong but had been either reluctant to share their opinion at the time or had not been listened to by their peers. This led to some fantastic discussions on listening to each other, respecting each other's ideas and opinions and ensuring children spoke up when appropriate. When things went wrong it was often discussed as a class, so they could learn from each other's mistakes and continue to develop their growth mindset.

"The language acquisition and development and social skills was astounding. Try to ensure your cooking area is in a quieter area of your classroom to allow for the incredible language that will come from it."

Cassie Smith, EYFS teacher, Decoy Community Primary School

Perhaps one of the more surprising outcomes during the project was how positive it was for children who would normally be reluctant to lead. Cooking gave them the chance to find their voice and they displayed confidence within this area of provision where they had not previously. These children often became the 'experts,' supporting their friends and showing their skills.

"It encouraged them to work as a team and listen to their peers. Some of the children really demonstrated their leadership skills and ability to support their peers. This was well highlighted by some of the shyer children who were able to teach and support their peers with measuring accurately."

Holly Skinner, Key Stage One lead, Year Two teacher, St Peter's Catholic Primary School

One of the more obvious benefits of snack preparation and cooking was the opportunity that it provided to experiment with food and explore food choices. They had the opportunity to learn the origins and traditions of food as well as basic food preparation skills and good hygiene

procedures. Many of the children recognised that they were learning valuable life skills and this promoted school/home links, with many children choosing to join in cooking at home or asking their families to repeat some of the recipes at home.

Giving children the chance to explore raw ingredients is an important tool for teaching children about healthy eating and fresh food. Through this project it was clear the children became more used to working with and tasting fresh fruit and vegetables as many of the recipes purposefully involve these to encourage the children to eat healthily.

"We had a child who is a really picky eater, thoroughly engaged in preparing his salad pot and then trying all the ingredients and running up to his mum at the end of the day full of excitement to tell her the foods he had tried. She was overwhelmed and amazed that such a simple thing could change his thoughts about food."

Helen Hope, owner, Norton Pre-School

With many settings choosing to grow their own food to use in cooking, it helps promote the understanding of how food is grown, where is comes from and the seasonal changes that affect food production. The cycle of planting food, picking it, cooking with it and then eating it provides a real learning experience full of possibilities.

The benefits I have highlighted and the learning experiences I have seen during this project, have convinced me of the tremendous impact of cooking provision. I could not have foreseen the amazing learning outcomes that this project would facilitate. The children's engagement, confidence and determination have astounded me. Their concentration, resilience and independence have shone through.

Upon completing the cooking project every setting and school involved has decided to keep their cooking area and will continue to use cooking and snack preparation as part of their provision.

About this book

I have created this book as a resource for Pre-Schools, Nurseries and Schools who want to introduce cooking particularly with 3- to 8-year-olds.

The book will consider how cooking and food preparation can promote the Characteristics of Effective Learning, cover areas of the EYFS and Key Stage One curriculum and beyond. It looks at cross-curricular learning and how cooking can be used as a starting point for learning as well as an enhancement.

It will give practical ideas for how to set up a cooking area, how to maintain the area and how to use it effectively to achieve the most successful outcomes. The emphasis is on creating areas which can be accessed independently during continuous provision. It includes 50 photocopiable recipes that the children can follow independently that can be selected according to individual needs.

This book aims to inspire teachers and practitioners to give cooking a try in their own setting. I hope it will give some idea of the impact that cooking, together with skilled adults, can have on provision and most importantly, the children.

Reference

Ephgrave, A. 2018. *Planning in the Moment with Young Children*, Routledge, Oxfordshire.

CHAPTER 2

Characteristics of Effective Learning

Introduction

Within all the settings, it soon became very clear that cooking provision actively promotes and encourages the Characteristics of Effective Learning. The Characteristics of Effective Learning look at how children learn and consider how children engage with their environment and other people. Development Matters (2012) states that these Characteristics "underpin learning and development across all areas and support the child to remain an effective and motivated learner." These Characteristics are:

▶ Playing and exploring
▶ Active learning
▶ Creating and thinking critically

In this chapter I will explore the Characteristics of Effective Learning and how they might be seen in cooking and food preparation. Although these Characteristics are identified within the EYFS, they can be applied to children within Key Stage One. It is still important to look at *how* children learn as well as *what* they are learning. If we set up a stimulating, purposeful and engaging learning environment then the children will have the chance to show us the skilled and motivated learners they are.

"Practitioners need to ensure coverage of the seven areas of learning and development over time. But what is absolutely essential is planning to create a rich, vibrant learning environment which supports children's own interests and supports the Characteristics of Effective Learning: an indoor and outdoor environment which motivates and engages children and supports the ways in which they think, helping them to develop their own 'tool kit' for learning."

Judith Stevens, *Observing, Assessing and Planning for How Young Children Are Learning*, edited by Helen Moylett, *Characteristics of Effective Early Learning*, Open University Press, Berkshire, 2013

"The cooking project supported the development of Characteristics of Effective Leaning in so many ways. From initially engaging children staying at an activity for longer than a few minutes to leading to them making links within their learning e.g. if one egg makes six cakes, how many will two eggs make? The children used the cake trays to work this out."

Hayley Simmons, EYFS leader, St Peter's Catholic Primary School

By observing children cooking, we notice the Characteristics of Effective Learning in some of the following ways.

Playing and exploring – engagement

Children are curious about the ingredients and tools provided. They use their senses to explore the food, touching, smelling, looking and tasting the raw ingredients as well as the finished products.

The children will often take the time in cooking to pretend the food they are working with is something else from their experience. This seems to be particularly more common with the malleable materials such as dough but can also be seen in the simple representation of a face when they are arranging their cut fruit or salad. They often represent their own experiences of cooking at home, using the opportunity to revisit the tricks and skills they may have seen. They become real chefs.

By leaving the cooking and snack areas open to the children we are leaving it up to them to initiate cooking. Giving them a choice of what is on offer to make that day is often a vehicle for seeing what the child initiates themselves.

The children know that the cooking area does provide challenge and dedication, but this does not stop them in any way from accessing it. They are happy to have a go at preparing new foods, even ones they might have never seen or tasted.

Active learning – motivation

As the recipes become more complex moving through EYFS and KS1, they require that the children stay focused for longer, more sustained periods of times. Even the simplest and shortest activity in EYFS requires the children to stay focused long enough to gather their equipment and ingredients, prepare their food and then tidy up after themselves. For example, when preparing toast, children have to:

▶ Put the bread in the toaster
▶ Wait for it to pop up
▶ Get a knife and butter
▶ Spread the butter on the toast
▶ Cut their toast
▶ Tidy up their equipment

This process is not lengthy, but it does require that the children see it through from start to finish in order to be successful. I have very rarely seen a child walk away from a cooking activity without finishing but I have seen many children remain focussed for an hour with a high level of fascination, working carefully and paying close attention to detail.

During cooking there are many times when a challenge will occur. The children might crack an egg on the table, they might put too much of one ingredient in or not enough of another and have to re-adjust as they work. They might add too much baking powder and their banana bread might collapse. All these situations require children to 'bounce back' and work together to solve the problem.

"One time I mixed up the sugar and the flour and it didn't taste very nice but the next time I made it I remembered to do it right and it was yummy!"

Reception child

Children are often keen to cook and show a huge amount of satisfaction when they have completed a recipe. You can see the delight and pride on children's faces when they have cracked their own egg or weighed an ingredient correctly.

"Having become interested enough to expend effort and energy in deep involvement and persevered even if things didn't go smoothly, active learners will continue to be drawn to learning experiences through receiving the satisfaction of reaching their own goals. This reflects the importance of intrinsic motivation where the experience brings its own reward."

Nancy Stewart, *Active Learning*, edited by Helen Moylett, *Characteristics of Effective Early Learning*, Open University Press, Berkshire, 2013

Creating and thinking critically – thinking

The children have to plan, make decisions and solve problems in order to reach a goal throughout cooking. They need to plan (often in that moment) who is doing what, how they are doing it and where it is going to be done. They need to make decisions regarding how long each process takes and whether they have finished that stage and are ready to move on e.g. have they stirred enough? Is the dough rolled thin enough?

It is fascinating to see how the children approach and solve problems as they work. Even the simplest food preparation requires the children to negotiate and make decisions. This could be anything from who is using the knife first to how to grate a carrot.

Children often adapt the recipes to suit their own likes and dislikes. They think of ways to present their products and even think of innovative ideas for products themselves. The children love to share these ideas with each other and build upon each other's ideas when working.

> "We noticed children using lots of their own ideas. They compared their own work with others, watching each other and borrowing/adapting their techniques and ideas."
>
> Stacey Hynd, EYFS lead, Thorley Hill Primary School

When cooking the children often make links between what they are currently making and what they have made in the past at school and at home. Making links to past experiences, they might predict what might happen to the product when it is put in the oven or the freezer or when ingredients are mixed together. They might be able to understand the use of products like yeast and be able to apply this to new recipes e.g. can they relate bread making to pizza dough?

It is so clear to see the Characteristics of Effective Learning in play when children are cooking, that it is easy to understand why teachers and practitioners felt the area was such a powerful resource for learning and development and have decided to keep it as an area of provision.

References

Stevens, J. 2013. *Observing, Assessing and Planning for How Young Children Are Learning*, Edited by Moylett, H. *Characteristics of Effective Early Learning*, Open University Press, Berkshire.

Stewart, N. 2013. *Active Learning*, Edited by Moylett, H. *Characteristics of Effective Early Learning*, Open University Press, Berkshire.

CHAPTER 3

Early Years Foundation Stage curriculum

Introduction

In this chapter I will explore how cooking and snack areas provide opportunities for children to learn across all areas of the EYFS curriculum. I will examine in detail how the recipes in this book and cooking itself can become an amazing addition to your enabling environment, introducing a wealth of rich experiences and new skills.

Prime areas of learning and development

This area of provision is fantastic for seeing the prime areas of learning at work. The children work together to develop their personal, social and emotional skills, language is a fundamental element and the area is very hands on, constantly developing their physical skills in different ways.

"Cooking was great for almost all areas of the curriculum but especially the prime areas. We were able to improve the fine motor skills of many of the children and the language acquisition and development of social skills was astounding."

Cassie Smith, EYFS teacher, Decoy Primary School

Personal, social and emotional development

Cooking and snack areas are naturally sociable therefore promoting positive relationships. It is clear to see children enjoying each other's company when cooking. Even if they are making an individual snack they will need the support of one another, sharing resources as they work.

It is common to see children working together, helping each other to overcome problems. This may be the simplest act of tying each other's aprons before beginning or holding the bowl when their friend is stirring. This extends to demonstrating skills to each other and explaining how to carry out a task. If children see their peers needing support they are often keen to help.

"Cooking is very inclusive. All children showed enthusiasm, independence and teamwork. One of the biggest benefits was the social aspect – their patience and encouragement of others."

Kelli Stocker, EYFS lead, St Michael's Church of England (VA) Primary School

When cooking, children will need to follow the rules/expectations set for this area and the children will often create their own rules and expectations as they work. In all the settings involved in this project, children have come up with many inventive ideas for working out roles and how to make everything 'fair' in their eyes. One group decided each child should stir for a count of ten and then move the bowl round. The responsibility given to them means that they often act with maturity.

"Children were encouraged to work in pairs or larger groups so between them they need to figure out how they will delegate roles and how they will ensure that everyone is getting a fair turn."

Victoria Farrelly, EYFS lead, Trekenner Community Primary School

In cooking, children can achieve something they are proud of. When they realise they can work independently to make a banana loaf or a potato salad, they also find they have achieved something great without the need for adults. This is fantastic for their confidence and self-esteem.

"The cooking area has developed the confidence of the children. It gave another area where children could excel in a skill set and develop different skills."

Hayley Simmons, EYFS lead, St Peter's Catholic Primary School

Physical development

The cooking area gives children the opportunity to put into practise the health and self-care aspect of physical development. They need to understand the purpose of hygiene procedures, how to follow them and what happens when they break down. The children can take responsibility for cleaning tables before beginning and after finishing. They soon get into good habits, washing their hands, rolling up their sleeves and if applicable putting on an apron. This becomes a natural part of cooking and snack preparation and during the project we saw children regularly reminding each other about these procedures.

"We used pictures to reinforce hygiene and safety. Children were able to bake independently but had to show that the area was clean, they were clean, the resources ready before they could. As with other areas this then became part of the routine and soon the children didn't need to have it checked. It became part of the process. When the children's Year 6 buddies came in lots of them wanted to bake cakes together and you could hear the Reception children running through the hygiene rules."

Hayley Simmons, EYFS lead, St Peter's Catholic Primary School

Through cooking, children learn to take and manage appropriate risks with equipment, using it and then storing it safely. If children have been taught to use the equipment with care and adults have demonstrated using the tools appropriately then the children will become more and more confident using them. Children being able to select and use tools with care is an essential part of the curriculum and teaches the children great life skills.

The children will have the chance to explore a variety of hand, arm, elbow and shoulder movements which help to develop fine and gross motor skills. These include: cutting, stirring, kneading, whisking, rolling, turning, lifting, cutting, tearing, pushing, pulling, twisting, pinching and pouring. These are embedded into the cooking process so remain purposeful rather than taking them out of context and practising them in isolation.

According to author Jan White, we should provide opportunities for holistic hand development.

"Experiences that develop awareness, feeling, dexterity and control in the hands involve using the hands in many different ways: to point, reach, grasp, grip, shake, stretch, squeeze, poke, squirt, hold, twist, hang, throw, stroke, smooth, press, pat, hit, bang, stamp, punch, stir, beat, pinch, pull, push, lever, sweep, brush, wipe, hold, handle, lift, carry, turn, mash, grind, whisk, and so on and on."

Jan White, *Every Child a Mover*, The British Association of Early Childhood Education, London, 2015

Communication and language

Within cooking provision, children need to follow instructions, listen to each other and explain their thoughts. They will use language related to sequencing and organising. This area will introduce children to new language including verbs, names of food and equipment and descriptive language. It is vital therefore that when the children are cooking adults make the most of opportunities to support communication and language. We have many chances to support language development in this context, from helping children to develop their ability to speak in complex sentences to introducing them to specific vocabulary.

Children will have the time to freely talk with their peers and express themselves. They will use talk to reflect and evaluate, to plan, to negotiate, to problem solve and to celebrate. This might be child/child talk or it might be adult/child talk, depending on the experience you have planned or the experience that evolves on that occasion.

Specific areas of learning and development

Literacy

Through the recipes and the labels on ingredients, children will develop their understanding that print conveys meaning and recognise some familiar words. They will use their phonic knowledge and initial sounds to decode. They will use reading cues to help them work out unfamiliar words in the recipes, using the context, thinking about what might make sense and using the pictures for support. They will gain a real sense of the language of instruction.

"We do reading. There's a special book we follow, there's instructions with pictures."

Reception child

Sometimes child led and sometimes on the suggestion of adults, the children have been inspired to use cooking as a starting point for writing. Children have chosen to write the recipes to take home when they have particularly enjoyed them or write shopping lists for their teachers and parents.

"Our biggest challenge was running out of ingredients! But this led to lots of writing opportunities. If/when we ran out of ingredients the children would write me a shopping list of the things we needed more of. This became part of the routine and was a good opportunity for children to write for a purpose."

Hayley Simmons, EYFS lead, St Peter's Catholic Primary School

We have found that children might have experienced cooking at home and want to share this recipe with their friends, so they have been encouraged to write their own recipes for others to follow.

One child who was inspired to write his own Yorkshire pudding recipe then carried out a cooking demonstration to the class. He wrote the recipe with a list of ingredients. The teacher shopped for the ingredients and the next day he shared his recipe under a visualiser, following it to make enough Yorkshire puddings for the whole class. This led to many other children writing recipes of what they liked to make at home including gravy and sandwiches.

To encourage frequent name writing, children can label their own bags to take home after they have cooked. Another simple idea is to have a clipboard in the cooking area for children to write their name when they have accessed the area.

The children particularly enjoyed writing a 'Top Tip' for other children and putting this on display for their peers. They often printed a photo to go with their tip.

There are many story books and poetry with cooking or food as a theme that you might like to have available for the children to read in a basket near the cooking area. There is also a large choice of non-fiction books about foods, where they come from, healthy eating, food from countries around the world and of course recipe books for inspiration.

Mathematics

There is huge potential for Mathematical Development through cooking. When cooking, children will encounter matching, counting and number, estimating, sharing and comparing, weight, measure and calculating, dividing and multiplying. In every session they will experience one or more of these mathematical concepts in a real-life context.

Counting and number

The children will have ample opportunity in this area to experience counting and number. Recipes in EYFS encourage children to count spoons or ingredients.

The practical nature of the area means the children can touch and move the ingredients. Not only will they have to count out specific ingredients for recipes but they can also count freely as they cook. They might count the strawberries or tomatoes or count the pieces that they have chopped a banana into.

Recipes might call for them to estimate number: how many strawberries will they need for their smoothie? Will it be the same number as the bananas? Why? Why not? There would be no wrong or right answer to this question, but it would require the children to think about number, capacity and volume in respect to what they were trying to create.

As many of the recipes involve number and counting, the children and settings have developed their own ways of recording as they cook to encourage accuracy. Some of the children have engaged in simple mark making and then tallying. Some of the settings have provided children with cubes and these have been used e.g. if there are ten spoonfuls then the adult will give them ten cubes so each time they put a spoonful the group can move one cube so they can keep track. They have used their fingers to keep track and used their fingers to move along a number line.

Some settings have used numicon within the cooking provision so that children can find the corresponding plate for each ingredient, some of them then placing the pegs in. Each setting finds ways to support the children and sometimes just leaving the equipment in the area can lead to interesting discussions.

Calculating

Addition

Addition can come into many aspects in cooking. A simple example is to think about how many pieces of fruit have been used on a rice cake e.g. I can see you have used three pieces of banana and four pieces of strawberry, how many pieces of fruit have you used altogether? This might come up naturally with the children themselves or adults might prompt this addition. It might be that you want to encourage thinking about this by displaying a maximum number of pieces of fruit for that day or recipe so children have to find ways of making that number.

Subtraction

This can be brought into cooking by adults working with the children. You have added three spoons of butter but only one of sugar. What's the difference? Or it might come up naturally with the children. I have observed children putting in too many spoonfuls of an ingredient and either noticing themselves or their peers have noticed which has led to discussions about 'now you need to take away one.'

Multiplication

The muffin tins which feature regularly in different recipes provide opportunities to look at and create arrays. It is fascinating to see how children arrange the cases within the tin and hearing their talk as they do so.

The children could experience repeated addition when they are cooking. They might do two spoonfuls each around the group and record this as marks to keep track. They might look at biscuits and work out how many they have altogether when they have made two each. Again this concept could come up naturally as children see patterns in number or it could be more explicitly pointed out by adults.

Sharing

Children encounter sharing when cooking through the ingredients. They will often share them up fairly round the group or they will divide the number of biscuits to give out to take home. They might divide their produce into pieces e.g. a pizza into three for the three members of their family or share dough into equal size pieces. They might cut an orange in half or a cake into quarters. The children pick up this language and use it correctly very quickly if they use it on a daily basis.

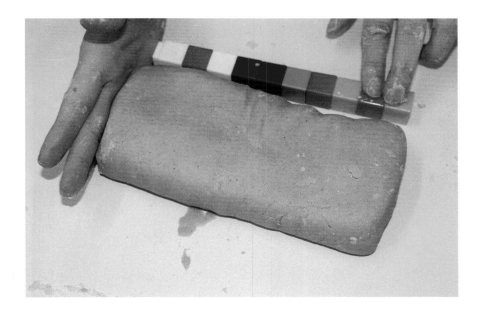

Shape, space and measure

Measure

Measure is linked with cooking in so many ways that children will gain plenty of experience with it through accessing the provision.

> "Measuring is a practical area of mathematics that must be learnt through hands on, meaningful tasks."
>
> Elaine Bennett and Jenny Weidner, *The Building Blocks of Early Maths*, Routledge, Oxon, 2014

Weight

In the cooking area, children will see and hold different containers/bags with a variety of weights such as a 1kg bag of sugar, a 250 g block of butter and a clove of garlic. Practical experience of holding ingredients will give the children experience of a variety of weights and through the recipes, they will begin to experience standard measure. They will use the balance scales when making cakes.

Capacity

It is helpful to have a variety of different size containers to encourage children to make choices between them according to their needs and desires. A few different size bowls or jugs will ask children to select the one most appropriate for the task. When using liquids in EYFS I might draw a line for the children to measure against or use tablespoons/teaspoons. Children who are ready to, might notice the numbers on the jug and this will introduce them to standard measure in ml. A group of children measuring liquid against a line will often discuss this at length, giving them an opportunity to use 'more' or 'less' in their discussion.

Accuracy within measure

"This is about children understanding that although they may make estimates when measuring, it is important that when using units of measurement they must work accurately. It is vital that children know why accuracy is important, for example inaccurate weighing when cooking could spoil the taste of a cake. Demonstrating how to use measuring equipment accurately, even when children are very young is therefore essential."

Elaine Bennett and Jenny Weidner, *The Building Blocks of Early Maths*, Routledge, Oxon, 2014

When teaching children to use teaspoons and tablespoons introduce them to the idea of 'levelling' the spoons to ensure accuracy. The idea that the spoons or cups always need to be full is a teaching point which comes up frequently but once children understand the importance of this it becomes a natural part of the process and they begin reminding each other.

Time

Cooking involves different measures of time, for example how long to wait for bread to rise or how long a smoothie takes to make compared to biscuits in the oven. This starts with the children experiencing what lengths of time feel like and could be extended to involve the standard measure of time, providing them with a means of timing for themselves e.g. tablets/iPads.

Sand timers could be added in the cooking area to see how the children might use them.

Cooking involves sequencing and putting instructions in the right order. Children soon see the importance of working in the correct sequence e.g. spreading butter must come after toasting.

Shape

Keeping some ingredients in their packets can be useful for shape as the children will see the 3-D shapes in packaging e.g. the cuboid in the icing sugar and butter and the cylinder in the baking powder. Adults will make the difference in this area, modelling language.

> "The mathematical language used to describe the properties of 2d and 3d shapes is often challenging for children. However, if this language is used by adults alongside their everyday vocabulary from a young age, children will begin to recognise, visualise and describe these shapes with much greater ease."
>
> Elaine Bennett and Jenny Weidner, *The Building Blocks of Early Maths*, Routledge, Oxon, 2014

A variety of 2-D shapes can be used with different shaped cutters which are used in a range of recipes such as jam tarts, cheese and tomato bites and biscuits.

Size and position

The recipes often encourage children to think about the position of the ingredients e.g. putting the icing on top of the cakes and might explicitly use this in their instructions e.g. 'make a well in the middle' or 'pour the milk into the bowl.' This encourages children to use positional language. This will also be used when finding equipment e.g. it is on top shelf. Displaying different size cutters naturally encourages thinking and discussion around the language of size.

Pattern

Several of the recipes naturally encourage children to create patterns. Children might create a pattern when making a salad, a fruit kebab, a fruit rice cake to mention just a few. The adults might take photos of the different patterns created for display or create a book for children to look through and copy or build upon.

Data handling

In its simplest form in cooking children will need to make choices. They will need to convey personal preferences and compare this to the rest of the group. They will then need to make a decision based upon this. For example, if choosing between a large cake and cupcakes how many children want each option? If three children want a large cake and one child wants cupcakes which is the most popular option? Does everyone want to add lemon to the cake? These questions will be ones which the children ask each other throughout and it is interesting to see how children approach these dilemmas. Children enjoy carrying out surveys to find out what the most popular choices for food are and these could be added to a cooking display. Children might instigate surveys before making a recipe e.g. how many children like garlic bread and how many children like cheesy garlic bread, or carry out taste tests after cooking.

Money

Money can easily be introduced into the snack/cooking area. It could be as simple as paying for a glass of milk by putting the correct coin in a pot or could be developed into paying for the ingredients to make their own fruit or salad and working out total costs.

Mathematical language

In the case of cooking the adults will have ample opportunities to introduce and model specific mathematical language.

> "The language children use in the early stages of measuring and comparing objects such as 'big' can only be developed into 'long' or 'heavy' or 'tall' by grasping every opportunity to model and rephrase their wording when working or playing alongside them."
>
> Elaine Bennett and Jenny Weidner, *The Building Blocks of Early Maths*, Routledge, Oxon, 2014

Through examining how many opportunities there are for children to experience these through cooking, we can begin to understand the huge learning potential there is for this area of learning.

Many mathematical ideas and concepts can be seen working alongside each other. Here is an example of how this might work:

> When making cupcakes the children will have to balance the ingredients. They will predict and choose how large a mixture to make depending on the eggs, they will have to work out how many cupcakes they can make, how much cake mix can be put in one cupcake holder and have they got the same amount in each? What kind of array should they use in the cake tin and how many they will each take home?

This cooking experience has therefore involved weight, estimating, capacity, number, multiplication and division.

> "There was a huge variety of Maths outcomes including fractions, number, comparing weight, length, shape and size etc."
>
> Stacey Hynd, EYFS lead, Thorley Hill Primary School

Understanding the world

People and communities

The cooking area could be used to explore traditional food from different countries and cultures or to explore traditional or favourite recipes from home.

> "The recipes in school have inspired lots of cooking at home which has then been shared back at school via Tapestry. It has opened up new conversations about comparisons with each other's home life and traditions."
>
> Stacey Hynd, EYFS lead, Thorley Hill Primary School

The world

Through cooking, children will have ample opportunity to experience changes, exploring change through melting, freezing, toasting and baking. These have led to interesting discussions and experiments. What happens if you put a lolly into the fridge instead of the freezer? How quickly does a lolly melt? Listening to children's discussions and questions will provide many starting points of learning.

Cooking is a fantastic resource for talking about ingredients and encouraging children to talk about where they have come from, how they are grown and their characteristics e.g. where does flour come from? What is inside a tomato or a pepper? What will happen if we plant apple pips? Children will naturally ask these questions and if encouraged they will experiment with this on their own, gathering their own resources and conducting their own investigations. These can of course be made into shared learning experiences for other children and enhanced by adult teaching.

A fantastic addition to a cooking area is a herb/fruit/vegetable garden. The children can watch their ingredients grow, nurture them and fully understand the growing process.

St Michael's C of E (VA) Primary School and St Peter's Catholic Primary have developed garden areas where the children can benefit from the experience of growing their own produce. A growing area might be vast or you might have a small outside area with raised beds. A herb garden creates new smells and sensations for the children to explore.

> We created a mindfulness garden using texture, colour, taste and smell. The herbs planted by the children are then used in cooking and each child has a free selection, deciding what they want to put in. We used it in Gazpacho soup, focaccia, herby scones, pizza bagels, hedgehog rolls and others.
>
> Over the year we have grown strawberries, pears, apples, green beans, tomatoes, potatoes, pumpkins, courgettes and marrows. The children learn how these grow and then use them in their cooking whether it be during an adult led activity or in their own independent cooking.

The children harvested the beans and potatoes to use the following year.

The children put the vegetable by-products of their cooking onto the compost heap so that they can replenish the soil.

We take the opportunity to use expressive language when in the mindful garden, linking it to senses, feelings and memories. This then transfers into reflective discussions the class have after cooking has taken place.

This year we have introduced bee feeders with sugary water so that we invite insects to come and drink, to give them energy during the hot weather. This has helped with discussions about the environment and valuing all creatures, linked to food sources and how we look after the environment. It has been great for life cycles and linked to seasons.

Maxine Idrissi, nursery nurse, St Michael's C of E (VA) Primary School

(continued)

(continued)

Originally whilst working in Reception I contacted a local charity organisation whose volunteers had worked with other schools to develop gardening projects.

They worked with us and the children to plant a herb garden and some plants that would encourage wildlife. The children loved using the herbs and adding them to their mud kitchen recipes so we then began using the herbs in our cooking area.

After witnessing this success, I contacted the volunteers again this year to help develop our KS1 gardening areas. They worked alongside the children during science week to teach them about plants and their needs.

In Year One we have a range of herbs, and in Year Two carrots, strawberries and potatoes, which were all requested by the children.

Having a gardening area has been a brilliant addition to our provision as the children have been extremely excited to watch our plants grow and pick them to use in our cooking area.

(continued)

(continued)

I feel it has been a fantastic way for the children to take ownership over their learning because they helped to plant and maintain our gardening areas. In Year Two we have a rota for watering and observing the plants changes and the children are always very excited when their name is on the rota.

Holly Skinner, Key Stage One lead, Year Two teacher, St Peter's Catholic Primary School

(continued)

(continued)

At St Peter's Catholic Primary School, the children in EYFS and Key Stage One have their own chickens to look after so they collect their own eggs.

A few years ago, our EYFS department hatched chicks from eggs as part of their spring topic but when the time came for them to return to the farm we found we couldn't part with them.

Our hens (in EYFS) provide many of the eggs that we need for our cookery across the six classes, however, this year we have established an additional flock of six hens who will live on the field near the KS1 classes, be their responsibility and provide them with all the eggs they need.

Understanding that the needs of our animals must come before their own needs teaches children empathy, responsibility and self-discipline – skills that they will need for their future learning.

Marianne McDonnell, deputy head, St Peter's Catholic Primary School

Technology

Children can use cameras or tablets to record their cooking, taking photos of the process or end product. This has been a useful accompaniment to encouraging children to write 'top tips' for each other for display. It is very quick for children to print off a picture to go with their tip and put it up instantly. Linked closely with time in Maths, they could use tablets, stopwatches and the clock to support timings.

They will be using a variety of equipment which supports ICT (with adult supervision) such as blenders, ovens and soup makers.

Expressive arts and design

The children often naturally add a design element to their cooking, exploring pattern and design. They often take on a role or create representations of objects from their experience. They can explore texture and extend their vocabulary of colour and form.

"The sugar is the shiniest and the flour looks hard but it is actually soft."

Reception child

"I like feeling the ingredients and taking it in turns to put them in."

Reception child

Example of learning

By looking in more detail at a one learning experience it is possible to realise the full potential of independent cooking in EYFS. Here is an example of how one bread-making experience can cover every area of learning as well as promote the Characteristics of Effective Learning:

> This is a short extract from a group of four cooking bread in Reception. The recipe has been available to the children for a while and the children have all had prior experience of making bread at school either working with an adult or independently. Today they work through the recipe independently from start to finish. The children have already begun making the bread and are currently adding the oil.

Making bread Reception

Child 1: is pointing to the recipe: Make a hole in the middle. It's got a hole. There you go. Now put the oil in the middle. It's (child's name) turn.

Child 2: carefully adds the oil and screws the lid back on: What's next?

Child 3: Put the water in the bowl.

Child 2: It says water? Oh yeah it says, 'pour the water into the bowl.'

Child 1: looks at the jug where a line has been drawn at the 200:200.

Child 2: That's really big. Where's the cup?

Child 1: It smells really nice. Ummm.

Child 2: It smells like bread. We can eat bread. Look at the line it needs a little more water.

They finish measuring the water together.

Child 4: Can I put it all in?

Child 1: Yes, put it all in, then mix. Have you ever made flapjacks? Once we made it but my mum left it in the fridge too long so we had to scrap it out. Now it's (child's name) turn. Then I think we are done.

Child 4: Then we have to leave it for one hour.

Child 1: We need to use our fingers to get it out. It looks really good.

Child 2: What's next?

Child 1: Put the flour on the table.

Child 4: I've done mine already.

Child 2: Now it's my turn. My hands are really dusty.

All the children clap their hands together and laugh.

Child 4: indicates towards the dough: You can get yours out.

Child 1: hands a piece to child 3. That's your bit.

They each take a lump of the dough and spend time checking they have a roughly equal amount by holding the dough next to each other.

Child 4: Look at what I'm doing. I'm rolling it in my flour. Do what I'm doing.

Child 2: I think I missed my flour because mine is sticky. I'll put more flour on.

Child 4: We have to knead it.

Child 1: I'm rolling it into a sausage. Look a sausage!

Child 4: That looks like a caterpillar. Mine is a burger. Yum yum yum! Mines a bit sticky. I need a bit more flour (puts some flour on) No more or it won't rise up. I'm doing it like my daddy showed me. Let's make a pancake. We like pancakes.

Child 4: starts singing: We like making pancakes! We like pancakes!

All children join in singing: We like making pancakes! We like making pancakes!

Whilst they sing they continue to play with and knead their dough. For approximately five minutes, they twist, stretch, push, throw onto the table, whack, bang, squeeze, pat and roll the dough.

Child 2: looks in the bowl: Look there's more in there.

Child 4: I'll get it off the spoon.

Child 1: I'm going to put flour on my hands so they don't get sticky.

Child 3: rolls a ball: Look at my ball.

Child 2: Mine is a mountain. Mine is the biggest.

Child 4: No they are equal. Mine is like a wrap.

Child 1: folds the dough: I'm going to fold it in half.

Child 4: Let's leave it now.

Child 2: Cook it in the oven.

Child 4: No we need to leave out for one hour. We need the oil (to grease the bowl).

Child 1: I will do that. I need a bit of oil and a tissue. Shall we smell our bread?

They all smell.

Child 1: Put it in the bowl for one hour. Mine's here.

Child 2: Mine's here.

Child 3: Mine's here.

Child 4: Mine's here.

They all put their piece of dough separately in the bowl.

Child 2: begins to tidy up: I'll put these back (ingredients).

Child 4: We need to wash up.

Child 1: In one hour we need to look and see if it is done. It is going to rise up a little bit but not as much as it is in the oven.

Child 3: We need to put it somewhere warm.

They look around the room and see the radiator and put it there. They continue to wash and tidy, returning to their dough about 45 minutes later when they knead it again then make it into rolls.

Characteristics of Effective Learning

Playing and exploring

Although the children have all made bread before they are happy to have another go and all show a positive attitude to the task, working happily together throughout, laughing, clapping and singing.

They definitely show a 'can do attitude' throughout. When playing with the dough the children take the time to represent their experiences and ideas. They use their touch to explore and feel and smell the dough.

Active learning

The children have all chosen to make bread and are enjoying taking part in the process. They take their time to enjoy what they are doing, playing with the dough and smelling it. They are working independently and not looking for support or reassurance from adults as they find this in each other. They solve challenges as they arise quickly and calmly, e.g. the dough being too sticky.

They work uninterrupted making their dough for over 45 minutes. They need no reminder to keep on task as they are all actively engaged throughout. They take their time and are not distracted by anything else going on in the learning environment.

Creating and thinking critically

As they cook, the children are making predictions about what might happen to the dough and discussing the process of the dough rising. They consider what will happen to the dough once it is on the oven and know from experience that the dough needs to be somewhere warm to help the rising process. They are using their past experience and adult teaching to make these links. They solve problems as they arise such as adjusting the consistency of the dough by adding more flour and taking water out of the jug when it is above the fill line.

Areas of learning and development

Personal, social and emotional development

The children demonstrate great negotiation throughout. There is not a moment in the whole process when the children need an adult to intervene to solve problems or designate roles. They listen to each other and show sensitivity to each other's needs.

Watching the children, you can see that they ensure every child is able to contribute. Throughout, they demonstrate their ability to work co-operatively as a group.

Physical development

The children are using tools and equipment throughout, demonstrating their understanding of how to use tools safely and with care. They are using their whole hand when playing with the dough, experimenting with movements and techniques, adjusting their grip on the dough and using heavy or light movements as they feel necessary. They look at each other's hand movements and mimic one another, trying new ideas.

When bagging their rolls later in the day, they all find the tying the white tag round the bag tricky, but they persevere until they have twisted it tightly, working on their fine motor skills.

As the children have had cooking experiences through the year they are aware of hygiene procedures and follow them closely. No one puts their fingers in their mouth, everyone remembers to wash their hands before and after cooking. They are careful to keep the food and flour on the table. They demonstrate a good understanding of safety when using the equipment. No one is closely monitoring or telling the children what to do but they all put the equipment away with lids on when they have finished with each tool or ingredient.

Communication and language

The children listen to each other as they cook. They listen to each other's ideas and share their own. They use past, present and future tenses and use talk to explain their thinking, organise and connect ideas. They are describing what they are doing using a range of verbs such as roll, knead and use some complex sentences using 'and' and 'because.'

Literacy

The children follow the instructions carefully, reading the words and pointing to them, using the photos for support. They turn each page as they need to and know they have to work in order. They look at the food labels. By following the instructions closely, they demonstrate understanding of what they have read.

When they have made their bread, the practitioner reminds them to put their rolls in a bag and they each write their name on a sticker to go on their bag.

Mathematics

Prior to this extract, the children use the recipe to carefully add the correct amounts of each ingredient. One of the children adds the flour and another child keeps track using their fingers. They repeat this for each ingredient, at one point using a tally on whiteboards.

They are aware they need to leave the dough for an hour and manage to estimate 45 minutes then find each other to come back and check, showing their developing sense of time and how to use it.

After making their dough, the children combine it before kneading and have to share out the dough equally between them again, which they do without any negotiation. Two children take a large piece and then spilt it in half with a friend. They talk about the size of the dough and use the words biggest, half and equal as they are using the dough.

When measuring the water, they are using a pre-drawn line on the jug but know this is 200 when they read it on the jug. They are developing their sense of capacity when they are filling the jug from the tap. They know that when measuring you need to be accurate and they must either add in more liquid or take some out.

Understanding the world

The children demonstrate a developing understanding of change over time, knowing the dough will rise then cook in the oven. They know that temperature affects whether the dough will rise. Whilst they cook, the children take time to share experiences from their home lives.

Expressive arts and design

They use the dough to explore ideas for creating such as making a caterpillar, mountains and they make up a song to sing whilst cooking. They spent time talking about the different textures and use words such as sticky to describe these.

This example of learning clearly shows the possibilities for learning within cooking. The high level of engagement and involvement means that the children are learning in a meaningful and memorable context. As shown in this chapter, cooking is a fantastic resource which can support all areas the EYFS curriculum.

References

Bennett, E. and Weidner, J. 2014. *The Building Blocks of Early Maths*, Routledge, Oxon.

White, J. 2015. *Every Child a Mover*, The British Association for Early Childhood Education, London.

CHAPTER 4

Key Stage One curriculum

Introduction

Cooking has many benefits in Key Stage One as well as Early Years. The recipes that appear later in the book have been created to reflect the needs of the children and the curriculum as well as create a smooth transition and continue to develop the Characteristics of Effective Learning.

The recipes are designed to be used within continuous provision or can be given as a set task so can be accessed whichever approach to teaching and learning is used. On a practical note if you have an approach to learning in Key Stage One which allows for independent learning/continuous provision, then it will make introducing cooking provision easier because the children will have the time to access it. They will also be more familiar with leading their own learning, working independently or with their peers. Using this approach enables children to have a wide variety of learning experiences in Key Stage One and many schools are now experiencing the benefit of using high quality continuous provision.

Introducing cooking provision throughout EYFS and Key Stage One clearly shows how continuous provision can remain challenging for each child and year group as they move through the school. The differentiation between recipes is so clear to see that it makes it easier to show teachers or leaders who may be reluctant to make the change from a more formal timetable, that introducing high quality continuous provision encourages high expectations during independent learning.

Cooking covers many different areas of the National Curriculum, as I will highlight in this chapter. A carefully considered approach can allow the children to use cooking as a tool for learning across many subjects. It can therefore be built into planning and given to a group during planned curriculum time. The following will provide some ideas about how cooking can be used as a learning tool in many different subjects and as a fantastic resource for cross-curricular learning.

"As children get older (especially in Year One), they can design their own dishes, writing ingredient lists and instructions, buy the ingredients, make the dish and then review the finished product."

Anna Ephgrave, *Planning in the Moment With Young Children*, Routledge, Oxfordshire, 2018

English

The children must rely on their speaking and listening skills when cooking. They need to interact with each other, listen to each other and explain their ideas.

> "The national curriculum for English reflects the importance of spoken language in pupils' development across the whole curriculum – cognitively, socially and linguistically. Spoken language underpins the development of reading and writing."
>
> National Curriculum in England, English Programmes of Study, Department of Education, 2014

They read the recipes, developing their understanding and comprehension skills. They develop a greater understanding of instructions. The more challenging recipes for Key Stage One have less photos and more challenging text. Children working together when reading and discussing meaning, gives them the chance to articulate their opinion, therefore valuing their ideas and asking them to reach shared conclusions.

In the Key Stage One classes involved in the project, they developed their own systems for using the cooking area which supported the children's development in reading and writing.

Some of the ways the teachers encouraged reading and writing were:

- ▶ Shopping lists
- ▶ Writing recipes (ones they had made and their own)
- ▶ Making class recipe books
- ▶ Writing top tips
- ▶ Labelling ingredients
- ▶ Posters to support healthy eating/nutrition
- ▶ Recipe evaluations and reviews
- ▶ Descriptions of food
- ▶ Researching the origin of ingredients
- ▶ Researching their own recipes from books or the internet
- ▶ Linking recipes to books e.g. Paddington Bear and marmalade sandwiches
- ▶ Posters advertising sales/events

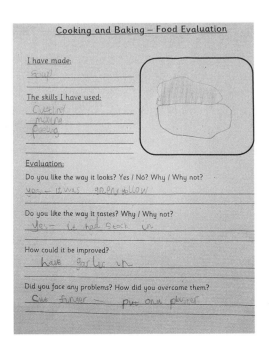

Method

1. First wash your hands
2. second peel banana and cut it
3. Next put the banana and the graips in the pot
4. Then maybee add water
5. After that Mix it
6. finally drink it

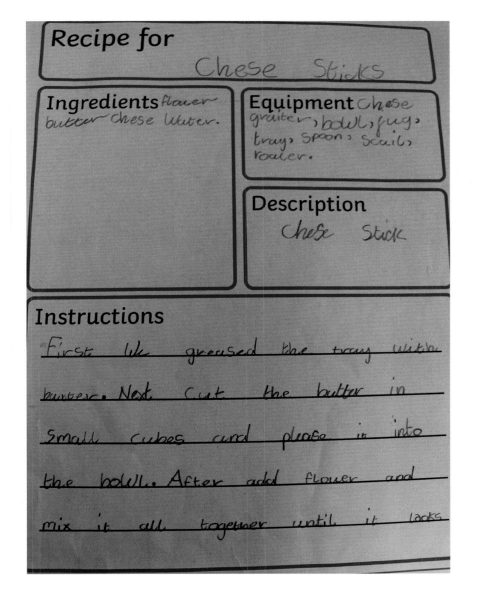

Recipe for
Chese Sticks

Ingredients flower butter chese Water.

Equipment Chese graiter, bowl, jug, tray, spoon, scails, roaler.

Description Chese Stick

Instructions

First lik greased the tray with butter. Next cut the butter in small cubes and please it into the bowl. After add flower and mix it all together until it looks

St Michael's embedded this into their practice so children who used the cooking provision would always have to write an evaluation of their products. Thorley Hill found that asking children to consider a current recipe and adapt it, write it as a recipe and then make it gave them a chance to write for a purpose.

> "It included speaking and listening, reading comprehension and instruction writing."
>
> Vittoria Townsend, Year Two teacher, Thorley Hill Primary School
>
>
> "It has developed children's reading skills. The children were encouraged to write their own recipe using suffixes."
>
> Holly Skinner, Key Stage One lead, Year Two teacher, St Peter's Catholic Primary School

Maths

The children will use the recipes to build upon their skills in number and place value, addition and subtraction, multiplication and division, fractions, measurement and geometry- properties of shape.

It may be useful to choose recipes that lend themselves to specific objectives. An example of this was St Peters linking their fraction learning to making pizzas.

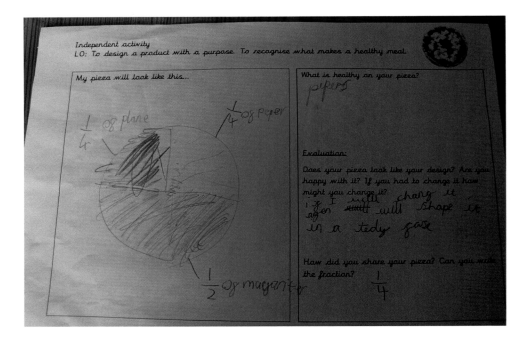

A cooking area naturally uses so much Maths but this can be extended to suit the needs of the class. Some of the ways you could use cooking to extend the children's mathematical skills are:

- ► Data handling/Surveys (research the most popular flavour of smoothies)
- ► Sales (put on a sale for parents)
- ► Buying ingredients (either from the shop or an online shop or a class shopping list)
- ► Working out costings and budgeting
- ► Problem-solving scenarios as a starting point:

    ▷ We only have three eggs but the recipe needs four. What should we do?

    ▷ If the recipe makes six cakes but we need 12 cakes, how much of each ingredient do we need?

► Timing recipes. The children can be responsible for the time the products are cooking for either using a stopwatch, a tablet or the class clock.

These could be one off learning opportunities for groups of children or some of these could be built into the expectations of using the area.

"The children used their measuring and problem-solving skills. We used multiplication and division to change the quantities."

Rachel Griffiths, Assistant Head, Year One teacher, St Michael's Church of England (VA) Primary School

"In Year Two cooking supported the Maths Curriculum – for measurement and capacity, division and sharing and fractions when cutting pizza."

Holly Skinner, Key Stage One lead, Year Two teacher, St Peter's Catholic Primary School

"Cooking included measuring, understanding of place value, reading scales, mass and capacity."

Vittoria Townsend, Year Two teacher, Thorley Hill Primary School

Science

The Key Stage One Science curriculum states that children should be taught to:

"Describe the importance for humans of exercise, eating the right amounts of different types of food, and hygiene."

National Curriculum in England, Science Programmes of Study, Department of Education, 2015

Cooking provision provides the perfect opportunity for children to explore hygiene and nutrition. Children could select and compare recipes to explore their nutritional value. They could use simple recipes such as making lemonade or orange juice to compare what they have made to shop-purchased products e.g. how much sugar is in one can of lemonade? The cooking area could make the perfect place to create displays to look at nutrition and healthy eating.

Many of the recipes explore a variety of fresh fruit and vegetables, giving choices within the recipes for children to explore their own tastes, likes and dislikes. Through the recipes they will be introduced to new ingredients, tastes and textures. You can explore this with them in so many ways e.g. making bread could prompt a discussion on different types of flour and the choices that are open to them.

Cooking can lead to many interesting discussions about the process of cooking and changing states.

"Through cooking, we explored the effects of heating and cooling, the process of change and the effects of raising agents."

Penny Hopkinson, Year Two teacher, St Michael's C of E (VA) Primary School

"We discussed the importance of healthy eating and identifying what is healthy for us."

Holly Skinner, Key Stage One lead, Year Two teacher, St Peter's Catholic Primary School

Design Technology

The Design Technology curriculum states that they need to explore ingredients and their characteristics.

> "Understand and apply the principles of nutrition and learn how to cook."
>
> National Curriculum in England, Design Technology Programmes of Study, Department of Education, 2013

The cooking area provides clear opportunity for this and gives children time to practise their cooking skills again and again.

> "The cooking area enhanced the Design and Technology curriculum. They did so much more having a cooking area than they would have done in a one-off cooking lesson."
>
> Sophie Turner, Key Stage One leader, Thorley Hill Primary School
>
> "We involved Design and Technology when making smoothies by designing and evaluating their end product."
>
> Alice Williams and Guy Barlow, Year One teachers, St Peter's Catholic Primary School

Design

The cooking area can be used to explore design. The children could be asked to design for a purpose e.g. a specific audience or event or they could design the product for themselves before beginning.

Make

Children will need to select appropriate tools when working from the equipment available for cutting, peeling, grating, rolling, joining, shaping, moulding and finishing.

The children will also have the opportunity to explore ingredients and their characteristics and select appropriately.

Evaluate

After cooking children could be asked to evaluate their product according to appearance and taste against their design or the design criteria.

These three elements can be incorporated in any recipe that the children use. If you wanted to create a particular focus on Design and Technology the children could be given a challenge related to this particular subject.

This example of a possible starting point for Design and Technology will give the opportunity for children to work across the curriculum, using their English, Maths, PSHE, ICT and Design Technology skills.

> Design a cake or cupcakes for a nursery child's birthday party. There will be 12 children at the party. The recipe you have makes six carrot cakes. Consider the flavours and appeal of your cakes. Your budget is £8.50.

The children could work together, visit Nursery children to find out their interests/likes/dislikes. They would then have to design the cakes, make them and evaluate them.

Computing

Computers and technology can be used as a tool to investigate recipes, present information and record cooking experiences.

In Year One at Thorley Hill, children used the smoothie recipe to make videos of themselves as TV chefs. They designed their own recipes then made them and after watching cooking videos they made their own.

"For computing, they learnt to video, looking at different techniques such as zooming. We linked it all to algorithms and the children were introduced to this concept in a very simple, familiar way."

Sophie Turner, Key Stage One lead, Year One teacher, Thorley Hill Primary School

PSHE

The themes and learning suggestions from the PSHE association clearly show how PSHE can be seen when using an approach which gives children time to learn with their peers. The association expects each school to create a programme of study for the needs of their unique children, but their programme of study does include Core Themes.

One of the PSHE Association's Core Themes is Health and Well-Being. As part of this theme they suggest that children learn:

▶ what constitutes, and how to maintain, a healthy lifestyle including the benefits of physical activity, rest, healthy eating and dental health
▶ to recognise what they like and dislike, how to make real, informed choices that improve their physical and emotional health, to recognise that choices can have good and not so good consequences
▶ how some diseases are spread and can be controlled; the responsibilities they have for their own health and that of others; to develop simple skills to help prevent diseases spreading

PSHE Education Programme of Study, Key Stage 1–5, PSHE Association, 2017

Cooking provision clearly reinforces this learning, providing the children with regular opportunities to demonstrate their understanding of healthy eating, making informed choices and their ability to follow hygiene procedures.

When the children are working together to create a product, they are developing their relationships with peers. They will be using these skills which feature in the Relationships theme.

▶ to listen to other people and play and work co-operatively (including strategies to resolve simple arguments through negotiation)
▶ to offer constructive support and feedback to others

PSHE Education Programme of Study, Key Stage 1–5, PSHE Association, 2017

The final Core Theme is Living in the Wider World. Using continuous provision in Key Stage One and in particular cooking provision, allows so many opportunities for the children to learn in a way which encourages them to have ownership over choices, work with peers and feel part of the classroom community. It suggests children should learn:

> ▶ how they can contribute to the life of the classroom and school
> ▶ to help construct, and agree to follow, group, class and school rules and to understand how these rules help them
> ▶ that people and other living things have rights and that everyone has responsibilities to protect those rights (including protecting others' bodies and feelings; being able to take turns, share and understand the need to return things that have been borrowed)
> ▶ that they belong to different groups and communities such as family and school
> ▶ what improves and harms their local, natural and built environments and develop strategies and skills needed to care for these (including conserving energy)
> ▶ that money comes from different sources and can be used for different purposes, including the concepts of spending and saving
> ▶ about the role money plays in their lives including how to keep it safe, choices about spending or saving money and what influences those choices
>
> PSHE Education Programme of Study, Key Stage 1–5, PSHE Association, 2017

Linking the cooking provision with Maths and budgeting could play a large part of this. The children could have a class budget and have to use it wisely or make more money when it runs out, possibly using their cooking skills. As mentioned for Maths, the idea of using money and how much things cost could be woven into the provision by having a price list for key ingredients that they could purchase in the 'school shop' or they might have to research the cost using the internet, writing not only a shopping list for ingredients but costing them beforehand to ensure they are within budget. The possibilities are endless and once routines and expectations are in place for using the area then the children will have opportunity after opportunity to consolidate their skills.

The following subjects are not going to always be covered using the cooking area but cooking provision can be linked to these subjects if desired. Here are a few examples:

History

Cooking could be linked to recipes from the past e.g. bread with the Great Fire of London.

> "Cooking bread fitted so well with our topic which was the Great Fire of London. Our role play was a baker's shop so it all fitted. The children enjoyed exploring all the different ingredients that can be added to the bread. Many tried herbs they had never, seen, smelt, eaten before."
>
> Vittoria Townsend, Year Two teacher, Thorley Hill Primary School

Children could find family members' recipes and explore how food and cooking has changed over time. St Peter's asked grandparents to contribute recipes of their own to school for the children.

"We shared family members' recipes and discussed how food and cooking has changed over time."

Holly Skinner, Key Stage One lead, Year Two teacher, St Peter's Catholic Primary School

Geography and religious education

Learning in the cooking area could be linked with traditional food found from a variety of cultures and countries. It could be used to explore food linked to religious festivals and celebrations. Many children have traditional recipes or family favourite recipes that could be re-created at school. The children could write these at home for other children to follow at school. Encouraging children to share in this way will help to build a community which respects each other and values each other's ideas.

"We made Simnel cakes linked to our RE and looked at the significance and history of these cakes."

Rachel Griffiths, Assistant Head, Year One teacher, St Michael's Church of England (VA) Primary School

Example of learning

Observing children from Year Two making muffins provides some insight into learning which might occur during cooking in Key Stage One.

This is the first time these two children have experienced making muffins at school and using this recipe. They are gathering their ingredients and equipment, checking they have everything they need to begin.

Child 1: What's baking powder?
Child 2: It's this.

They continue to fetch ingredients using the list until they have everything they need.

Child 1: reads the recipe and prepares the banana: It says mash banana. We need to weigh the banana. We need 225 g. (Puts one on the scales.) We need another one I think, this is 198 g. (Adds another banana) 306 g. What about if we half it? (Halves the second banana). 247 g. How many do we need? (checks recipe). 225 g. 227 g it is now. That's close enough I think.
Child 1: Now we need to mash it. What do we mash it with?
Child 2: With a fork.

They decide to eat the left-over bits and smile at each other.

Child 2: Let's wash our hands after so the germs don't go on the other bits.

They continue mashing the banana together.

Child 1: I quite like doing mashing. It's fun!

They add and mix the other ingredients, stirring them in.

Child 1: I hate doing egg! Why don't we do it into a cup so we can take the shell out if it goes in?

They drop a little shell in and get it out with a fork and then their fingers.

Child 1:   I've touched raw egg, so I need to wash my hands.
Child 2:   We've done the egg so now we need to do the water. I've already measured it.
Child 2   *pours in the water from the jug:* Ok now oil. How much oil do we need?
Child 1:   125 ml.
Child 2:   points to a line on the jug: That's about to there. Shall we do it to there? Tell me when its ready and I'll pour. Is it ready?
Child 1:   No, it's not right yet.

They decide it is correct and pour it in.

Child 2:   We need another bowl to put in the flour. Let's use this little one.

They put the bowl on the scales and zero it.

Child 1:   How much do we need?
Child 2:   225 g Oh, come on it's 250!

They laugh and take some out. They read it at 224 so they add some and get 227. They reach a decision to leave it there.

Child 1:   We should have left it at 224 it would have been closer. Can we mix it?
Child 2:   No, we need 1 teaspoon of bicarbonate of soda and the baking powder.

They add the baking powder then begin adding the bicarbonate of soda.

Child 2:   Oh, I've done half a teaspoon. How many do we need? 2¼.
Child 1:   adds 1 half: So, add another half that will make 1 then another 2 halves then a ¼.
Child 2:   adds 1 half: 1 more half in and that makes 1 and a half.
Child 1:   So, we need 2 and ¼ teaspoons so we need to add another half and then a ¼.

They do this together working very concisely with the spoon measures.

The teacher walks by at this moment and Child 2 tells her: Because we want different things, we are going to halve it. I want raisins and she wants blueberries.

Teacher: How are you going to half it? How are you going to go about it?
Child 1:   We could weigh it or we could just do it with our eyes.
Child 2:   We need to halve it on the table, so we need to put flour down.
Child 1:   No, we don't put it on the table. We need another bowl.

They spend some time mixing.

Child 1:   It takes forever to mix it! Let's halve it in the bowls now.
Child 2:   We are going to estimate.
Child 1:   Or we could weigh them.
Child 2:   Let's just estimate because the bowls are different weights on the scales. Use the big, big spoon to split it.
Child 2:   splits the mixture between the bowls.
Child 1:   How is that the same as that? (laughing) I need more!
Child 2:   (also laughing): OK you can have a bit more.

They continue, halving their mixture, adding their own ingredients and putting it in their cupcake cases. They ask an adult to put it in the oven and use the I-Pad to time how long it goes in for. As they wait for it to cook they wash and dry up independently without prompting.

Learning

The children are negotiating, listening to each other, questioning each other and challenging ideas in a friendly and supportive manner.

They are using the scales and demonstrate an understanding of using these to weigh accurately in grams. They adjust the weight by adding and taking away, showing an understanding of the place value. They use their knowledge of capacity to measure the oil and the water, again making sure that they measure accurately. They estimate throughout, with the banana, the mixture and the number of raisins or blueberries they need.

They read and follow the instructions together. During the cooking session they show their understanding of the need for hygiene and care by washing their hands when needed as well as storing the equipment and food safely when they are working.

Observing this brief interaction and learning experience, it is noticeable that the children are all solving problems, thinking independently and applying their knowledge and understanding from a variety of learning experiences from both school and home.

What I notice most when observing these children cook and interact with each other is the engagement they have with what they are doing and the relationships they are developing with each other. Observing their kindness, consideration and willingness to work together, support and challenge each other is fascinating and demonstrates to me the need there is to provide opportunities for children to work collaboratively.

In this chapter, I have explored just some of the possibilities for learning through cooking in Key Stage One. Cooking naturally covers so much in a real-life context that it is a powerful addition to any classroom. The challenge or recipe you use can be chosen according to the areas of the curriculum that you would most like to address and this can be clearly shown on planning if required. It is easy to adjust the learning experience to one which suits the needs of your cohort of children or indeed specific children so that you are creating a targeted challenge. The benefits of allowing children time to problem solve, work together and achieve independently cannot be underestimated.

Reference

Ephgrave, A. 2018. *Planning in the Moment with Young Children*, Routledge, Oxfordshire.

CHAPTER 5

Introducing cooking provision

Introduction

In this chapter I will explore how cooking can be introduced into provision. This includes questions you might like to consider before starting out, which recipes to use, how to maintain the area and encourage independence as well as safety tips and suggestions. It will also consider what teaching might look like when cooking.

How to get the best out of a cooking area

Before introducing cooking into your provision, it is helpful to have a team discussion to determine how you intend to approach this. This will ensure a consistent approach and hopefully help everything go smoothly. Some questions you may want to ask as a team before you begin are:

▶ How can we introduce cooking so it creates realistic but challenging provision for our class?
▶ What do we want our children to gain most from this provision?
▶ How can we as adults support the children in the most effective way?
▶ How independent do we expect the children to be and how can we facilitate this?
▶ How will adults support/teach children in this area?
▶ How can we ensure that the area is the highest quality provision we can offer and how can we ensure that the highest quality teaching is happening?
▶ How will we fund the ingredients?

There is no one answer to these questions as they will be individual to each setting but hopefully the following advice and tips will help you to find your own answers.

Starting out

It is important to consider the starting point of your children. How much experience have the children had with cooking and food preparation? How accomplished are they at accessing areas of provision and then tidying as they play? Tidying up is a massive part of cooking and expectations need to be established from the start.

The answer to these questions may determine how confident you feel or how appropriate it may be to leave the children to work independently or how much you need to demonstrate and model before they become independent.

If you want the children to use the cooking area truly independently, they need to be aware of the whole cycle of cooking. At first when preparing simple foods for snack you might only expect the children to wash their hands, prepare their snack using equipment and ingredients provided and set out for them, eat their snack and then wash their plate and cup.

As the recipes become more complex, the cycle becomes more complex. The children will now be washing their hands, finding their equipment and ingredients, following the recipe, washing up the equipment, putting it away and cleaning the table ready for the next group.

There is value in encouraging the children to take responsibility at an age-appropriate level. It teaches them good hygiene procedures and really lets them take ownership of their environment. The children often enjoy washing, drying up and cleaning the table. It gives them another opportunity to use their gross motor skills and a variety of physical movements e.g. a wrist pivot for washing and drying a bowl, an elbow pivot when cleaning the table, a shoulder movement when sweeping the floor.

It is important that this cycle is taught from the beginning otherwise the children will leave the area messy and it will need adults to spend time cleaning up and tidying after the children, preparing the area for the next group. This will interrupt adults who are likely to be involved with other children within a different area of provision. If children are taught this cycle and can follow it independently then the area will look after itself.

St Michael's found they wanted to embed the cycle and introduced the children to a flow chart to help them see this.

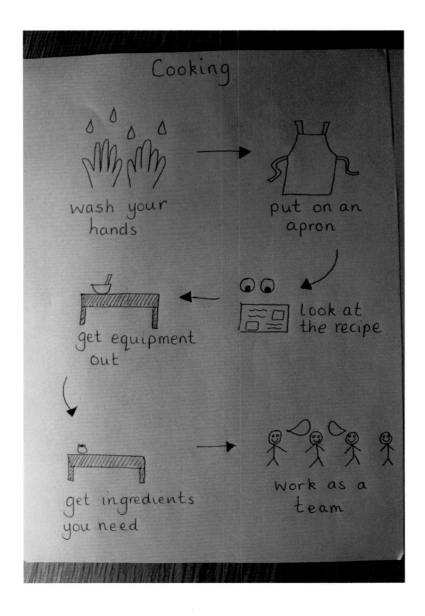

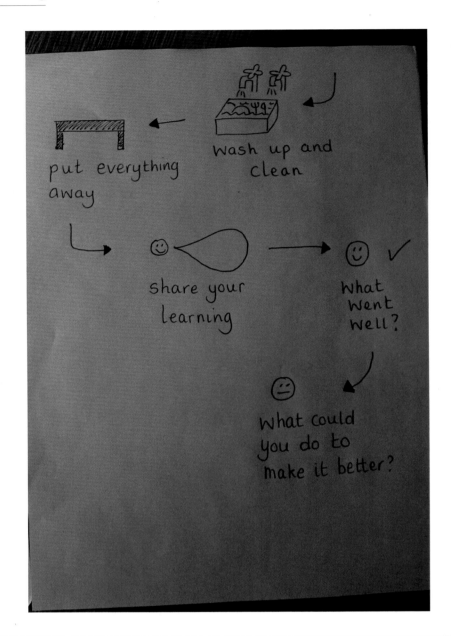

"At beginning of the year, we modelled it to each child as we wanted them to all be taught the whole cooking cycle e.g. washing hands, cleaning area, cooking, clearing up afterwards etc. As the children became more familiar with this and had more skills we would model it to one group and then let the other children become teachers to other groups."

Kelli Stocker, EYFS lead, Reception teacher, St Michael's Church of England (VA) Primary

Safety in the cooking area

When children start cooking there will be elements which may make adults anxious and which may pose risk to the children. It is important to reach a consensus amongst staff as to how confident you feel leaving the children with tools and be sure you are that the tools you are using pose a minimum risk to the children.

Are the knives safety knives? Do the children know how to use a grater safely? Is the blender out of reach of the children? Are there any other risks to consider?

Sharing a risk/benefit assessment with all staff and volunteers is essential so that all adults know the expectations of using equipment and how to ensure minimum risk and maximum benefit. For guidance see Risk/Benefit Assessment at the end of this book, but please note that this will need to be adapted to your own setting.

One really useful exercise is to conduct a risk assessment with each class as you introduce the area. Are the children themselves aware of the risks and how to manage them? Giving children ownership of the area and having this discussion promotes health and self-care. As new equipment is introduced this may need to be modified.

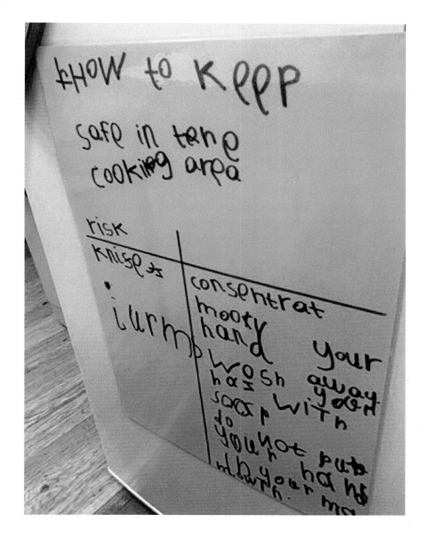

"Note that before you start anything go through your equipment and how to use it safely so that you can feel comfortable when they work without you. We did some whole class training on using knives and then a one to one with each child so that we could check technique. We posted this on Tapestry and encouraged parents to continue to support these skills at home."

Stacey Hynd, EYFS lead, Reception teacher, Thorley Hill Primary School

Make sure that you are all happy with the equipment you have selected. Choose knives you are comfortable with. There are several children's safety knives on the market or you may choose to use table knives for some foods (though using these knives will not be suitable for a lot of fruit and vegetables and may cause frustration and possibly more accidents). You need to make sure the knife is safe for the children to use independently and that you are comfortable with your choice. You must be confident that you have established safety rules with the children.

When selecting other equipment there are differences that might affect the safety e.g. one apple corer might have an elevated handle to keep fingers away from the blade where others will not have this feature and make it far more likely that the children cut themselves. So consider everything carefully when you are setting up your provision.

> "We have purchased some child-friendly knives which had a zig-zag blade. At the start of the cooking project, and any cooking prior to this, we have always ensured we have modelled and checked children's strategies for using the knives. This gives us an opportunity to teach the children in the moment and step back to allow children to explore the recipe independently."
>
> Victoria Farrelly, EYFS lead, Trekenner Community Primary School

There are a few useful methods to know when teaching children how to use equipment safely. After demonstrating and letting children have a go themselves, it is really helpful to take a photo of a child using each method for display as a reminder.

Breaking methods into simple steps will help them to remember the techniques.

When teaching children to use knives, one useful method for food such as potatoes and strawberries is the '**bridge method**.'

1   Make a bridge over the food with your hand. Your thumb should be on one side and your fingers on the other side.
2   Guide the knife underneath and then back out again like a train going in and then out of the station.

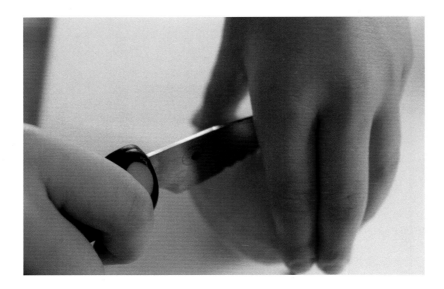

When using knives to chop foods such as celery and banana, you can teach children the '**claw grip**.'

1   Put your fingertips on the food like an animal claw and press down to stop it from moving.
2   Keep you knuckles facing the knife and slide them back as you are cutting.
3   Remember to keep fingers vertical and the thumb well back.

When **peeling** food such as carrots it is important that the children realise the peeler is sharp.

1   Put the carrot flat on the chopping board and hold at one end.
2   Start half way down and run the peeler along the length of the carrot in a direction away from yourself.

When **grating** food again remind the children that the grater is sharp.

1   Hold the grater firmly by the handle.
2   Grate the widest side, running it down and up firmly.
3   There is no need to continue until the end. Stop when you have a small chunk left.

Don't forget that there are some foods the children will be able to tear and cut with scissors and in some cases the children might find this easier. The children need to keep their fingers away from the scissors and when cutting small items such as herbs you can teach them to put the herbs in a cup and cut the herbs inside the cup so their fingers are always on the outside.

You could start off the preparation for them in some cases and let them continue. Most importantly make sure you have prepared the children and are prepared yourself in knowing the skills that the children will need for each recipe. Not all recipes will require all techniques so when the children need new skills or to use new equipment it might be necessary to model these to the children.

"We sometimes taught particular skills separately in a mini master class, so that the children knew how to chop safely, grate carefully etc. This helped us assess whether the children were ready to work on a recipe independently."

Kelli Stocker, EYFS lead, Reception teacher, St Michael's Church of England (VA) Primary

Level of challenge

All children and cohorts will bring different experiences to the provision. The recipes in this book have been created progressively to suit both the EYFS and National Curriculum. It is important that you select recipes that you feel match the needs of your children. The recipes you choose should be accessible to the children and manageable yet not so easy as they provide no sense of struggle or achievement.

"It is only from meeting a challenge just beyond what we can currently do that we have the opportunity to develop new skills and understanding, and this carries a built-in risk that we won't be successful in our efforts."

Nancy Stewart, *Active Learning*, edited by Helen Moylett, *Characteristics of Effective Early Learning*, Open University Press, Berkshire, 2013

It may be that you have some children in Reception that you would like to experience standard measure in grams or it might be appropriate, especially in the beginning of Year One, to use some of the EYFS recipes to continue to allow for independence. The most important consideration is what is going to work for your class and for the adults so look at each recipe closely and consider whether it is the right level of challenge for your children.

You might choose a recipe to help the children develop a particular skill or a recipe that you feel will suit their interest at that time. The recipes can be adapted for this purpose and this should be encouraged with the children.

Working independently and managing provision

Once you feel confident that the children can manage the area and use the equipment safely, the cooking and snack areas are great areas for the children to work independently.

In Nursery/Pre-School many of the recipes need fresh ingredients and once the children become familiar with a few of them, the EYFS recipe cards could be left out for the children to browse and select as needed with the snack/food preparation area. A selection of fruit and salad, together with the recipe cards, will lead to an open-ended snack area where children are expected to think for themselves and create a dish which suits them. This offers much more engagement and challenge than an area where children select one piece of fruit and eat it.

"The biggest benefit for us has been the snack area has become a place to learn and explore, not just a place to eat and drink quickly."

Louisa Cowler, Owner and Manager, Sunflowers Pre-School

"I was surprised at how well they managed and how little support they needed to prepare their snack."

Louise da Costa, Nursery Teacher, Thorley Hill Primary School

In Reception, the snack area could remain similar to this in set up so the children could build upon their Nursery/Pre-School experience and then you might introduce a separate cooking area if you have space.

Once you have introduced a cooking area and the children have experienced a few recipes, you will need to consider whether you want to have one recipe on offer or whether you would like the children to be able to choose from a variety. This is more complex as the children will have more ingredients and equipment to choose from.

If you are confident with this, the recipes can be left on display so that children can move between them as they wish. The difficulty here is often the cost and replenishment of ingredients. One solution is to offer a selection of recipes with similar ingredients. For example many of the baking recipes use similar ingredients so a way to still offer choice and make ingredient shopping more manageable is to keep a core of baking ingredients so that children can move between cakes, biscuits and bread.

In Key Stage One so many of the recipes are open-ended that there will be a choice within the recipes. When making bread the children have so many choices. Will they use white or wholemeal flour, will they add herbs, what shape will they make, will they add any other ingredients? It may not be possible to offer much choice between many recipes for practical reasons but it will be possible to still offer lots of choice within them.

After introducing a new recipe, the same recipe might last for weeks as the children return to it time and time again, often choosing to work with different children. As their confidence and skills grow, they will often become more creative so no one cooking experience will ever be the same.

When you observe the children working with their peers in the cooking area it is clear to see the impact that this provision has on their confidence and problem-solving skills as well as how fantastic it is for their relationships. They gain so much from the experience of cooking independently that sometimes, although it might be tempting to step in when they have found a problem, try to stand back for a while to observe and see if they can work through problems without adult support.

"Too many people still believe that children who are learning alone are somehow missed out and that their experiences are in some ways deficient. Nothing could be further from the truth. There are times when learning alongside an adult is the most efficient way to learn and times when an adult inhibits what needs to be learned."

Julie Fisher, *Interacting or Interfering*, Open University Press, Berkshire, 2016

When the children are cooking independently there may be times when teachers and practitioners observe the children and spot teachable moments where they can make a difference and offer direct teaching which they feel *will* benefit the group.

It is then worthwhile considering the type of interaction and teaching the adult will bring into the situation. The Ofsted definition of teaching is a useful resource when talking with adults about their role in the area.

"Teaching should not be taken to imply a 'top down' or formal way of working. It is a broad term which covers the many different ways in which adults help young children learn. It includes their interactions with children during planned and child-initiated play and activities: communicating and modelling language, showing, explaining, demonstrating, exploring ideas, encouraging, questioning, recalling, providing a narrative for what they are doing, facilitating and setting challenges."

OFSTED, 2018, EYFS Inspection Handbook

In this table I have outlined just a few examples of how each of these teaching strategies could be used in the cooking area.

Table 5.1

Strategy	Example
Communicating and modelling language	Adult cooking alongside the children "I think I might grate my carrot rather than cut it. I need to move it up and down."
Showing	Adult shows the children a grapefruit "Have you seen one of these before? Would you like to feel it? I wonder where it comes from?"
Explaining	"The grapefruit grows in hot countries like South America. It grows of trees just like grapes in bunches."
Demonstrating	"This is how you use a knife safely" (demonstrates using a knife safely to the child).
Exploring ideas	"I wonder what would happen if we put the lolly in the fridge rather than the freezer?"
Encouraging	"I know you can mix those ingredients really well so they bind together, maybe you could mix a bit harder."
Questioning	"How did you make the cucumber that thin? I wonder if we could do the same to the pepper?"
Recalling	"I remember what happened to the dough when we made bread."
Providing a narrative	"I can see you have weighed that very carefully and remembered to zero the scales with the bowl on."
Facilitating	"Would you like to add some decorations to your carrot cakes? Shall I show you where the decorating equipment is?"
Setting challenges	"I wonder if you could double this recipe so we could have more biscuits?"

These are simple examples of teaching that might happen in the cooking area but will hopefully give an idea of the scope for learning and challenge that it provides.

Children as teachers

One method that schools involved in the cooking project found successful was for teachers/practitioners to work a new recipe with a group of children and then use those children to teach the next group and so on. This obviously saves the teachers from having to go through the recipe with so many groups and also gives the children the opportunity to become experts, boosting confidence and self-esteem.

"We initially would talk through the stages of a recipe together and an adult would model to one or two groups. This would then lead to children who would be our 'Master Bakers' who had really grasped the concept, teaching other members of the class. If a less confident baker wanted to bake they were signposted to a 'Master Baker' who would be able to support them."

Hayley Simmons, EYFS lead, St Peter's Catholic Primary School

"An adult taught the first group, who usually taught a group of three to four children. Then one or two taught the next group. Some children emerged as natural teachers. These children were then called upon if things started to go pear shaped with some groups. I would say that the teacher never had to wash their hands because they never touched anything. This seemed to remind them to not be too hands on."

Alice Williams and Guy Barlow, Year One teachers, St Peter's Catholic Primary School

"The children had previous experience of cooking in Year One so I didn't feel the need to model first. I read through the recipes with them and we addressed issues as we went. The children were able to work really independently with the recipe cards. For those children who needed support with the reading we introduced a sous chef. The children cooking were the head chefs but they could go to the sous chef for help if needed. This worked really well."

Vittoria Townsend, Year Two teacher, Thorley Hill Primary School

The experience of introducing cooking into your provision can be challenging but it is so exciting and rewarding once it is established. When you observe the children cooking as a group without adult support, working collaboratively and applying all their skills and knowledge it will be worth the time and effort it has taken.

References

Ephgrave, A. 2018. *Planning in the Moment with Young Children*, Routledge, Oxon.

Fisher, J. 2016. *Interacting or Interfering*, Open University Press, Berkshire.

Stewart, N. 2013. *Active Learning*, Edited by Moylett, H. *Characteristics of Effective Early Learning*, Open University Press, Berkshire.

CHAPTER 6

Setting up a cooking area

Introduction

In this chapter I will look at the practical options for setting up a snack area and/or a cooking area. There are lots of possibilities for this, depending on the space you have available and the type of environment you want to create.

Snack area, cooking area or both?

In Nursery and Pre-Schools as the foods that the children are preparing are often simple and can be eaten immediately for snack, I would recommend having a larger snack area that the children can use to prepare and then eat their own snack. This area could be as extensive or as simple as you like. You will need a jug for milk and water and cups. Jugs give children the responsibility for pouring their own drink and washing up their cup afterwards. The washing up could be done in a nearby sink or if you don't have this handy, a washing up bowl prefilled with soapy water and a simple draining area will suffice. If you encourage them to put the equipment into the bowl as they finish with it, it keeps the area tidy and easier to use.

As a simple start for snack preparation, the area might have a selection of fruit and vegetables with chopping boards, safety knifes or table knives (depending on food) and bowls/plates. This way the children are always expected to prepare their own snack and develop their physical skills.

Once the children are familiar with this snack preparation, the recipe cards can be added together with the relevant equipment. You could introduce one recipe card at a time e.g. fruit faces and then either change this for another recipe e.g. salad pot or give children the choice of several cards. As the children become familiar with these recipes they will often recreate them or make a combination of them. These snack recipes are great for introducing children to new foods and encouraging them to eat a variety of fruit/vegetables daily.

A snack area could also include a simple cereal and/or toast stations. These could be a constant addition, an enhancement or added just one day week. These stations are another good way for the children to develop their physical skills and give them more choices about their own food.

A toast or cereal station is the perfect way for children to be involved in preparing their own snack. A toaster can obviously pose a risk, so it is important to risk/benefit assess this first as a staff and then with the children. Involving children in assessing the risk and asking them to help make safety rules helps to ensure that the children know the risks involved. Ashleigh Primary School asked the children to make signs to surround the toaster reminding their peers not to touch and wait until the toast pops.

It is so easy to set up a toast and/ or cereal station as all you need is a toaster and some spreads or cereal in containers and a jug of milk. You could add yoghurt or fruit to chop as toppings if you would like to explore healthy eating or encourage more design into the process. The toast station could explore different types of bread. A voting sheet could be put up so that children can vote for their favourite bread or topping. These stations will evolve with the children as they think of their own ideas.

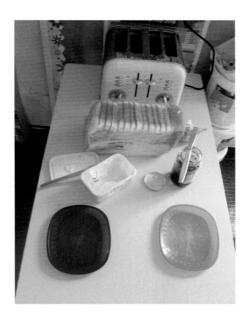

In Reception I would recommend continuing a snack area in the same style but adding a cooking area. As the recipes become more complex and need more equipment and ingredients, the children will find it difficult to cook and eat their snack in the same place.

In order to make best use of the cooking area it does need its own dedicated area in the classroom. You need to consider how much space you would like to or can dedicate to the area. I would suggest the cooking area needs to ideally be large enough for 4 children. A maximum of 4 children works well and seems to be effective for children working collaboratively. Having a workspace that the children work around allows the children to communicate with everyone in the group.

"When setting up the cooking area, I think it is important to know that you don't need a huge amount of space. Our cooking area started off as one table and 3 shelves where we had our equipment. This did evolve over time and depending on the number of children who wanted to access cooking within the provision we would add or take tables away."

Hayley Simmons, EYFS lead, St Peter's Catholic Primary School

Again, having a washing up/sink area next to the cooking area is useful but if this is not possible then a washing up bowl to put the equipment in as the children work is an essential addition.

Spoons

One key part of the recipes is the differentiation between teaspoons and tablespoons. Without children knowing the difference it can cause difficulty, but the children discussing the difference can encourage lots of mathematical talk. I have found the easier way to help the children remember the difference and use the recipes is to colour the spoons and mark the recipes with the corresponding colour. But also, to talk about them explicitly with the children and encourage them to hold them next to each other to see the difference. The children could make their own poster to show the difference.

Equipment

If you are setting up a new area, you will need to have some equipment ready. Here is a basic list of equipment you will need for the recipes in the book. Of course, you do not need all this equipment to begin but it is helpful to have everything you might need in place.

Bowls (a few varied sizes)
Teaspoon
Tablespoon
Metal spoon
Wooden spoon
Grater
Peeler
Fork
Dinner knife
Chopping knife
Chopping board
Baking tray
Muffin tin
Loaf tin
Scissors
Rolling pin
Hand juicer
Lolly moulds
Ice tray
Balance scales
Digital scales
Cake cases
Greaseproof paper
Garlic press
Mortar and pestle
Cake tin
Cake tray
Colander
Shape cutters
Jug
Measuring cups
Baking beans (Year 2)

"Initially make a list of all the equipment needed and then buy this for each class so they have a set of equipment. Make sure the areas are organised and keep de-cluttered."

Holly Skinner, Key Stage One lead, St Peter's Catholic Primary School

Cooking equipment

Oven
Microwave
Blender
Soup maker
Toaster
Frying pan

(Don't worry if you do not have all of these, you can pick and choose from the recipes)

Helpful extras

Apple corer
Melon baller
Spiraliser
Aprons

"You don't need a lot. We used digital scales which worked well with Year One. A lot of it was sourced from Poundland, so very cost effective. You need to find a secure way of storing ingredients that are not kept in the fridge. We also provided the children with a washing up bowl, cloth etc so part of their cooking is clearing up after themselves."

Alice Williams and Guy Barlow, Year One teachers, St Peter's Catholic Primary School

Scales

For EYFS you will need balance scales for the cakes but it might be also be useful to have some weighing scales showing grams and kilograms.

Schools found using digital scales useful for some of the recipes as they were more accurate but also had analogue scales available. If you would like children to focus more on how to make amounts then brass scales with weights are a fantastic resource and work well.

Storage

In terms of storage or shelf space, you will need to consider whether you would like to offer one recipe at a time or whether you would like (in time) the children to be able to move between several recipes. This will affect the amount of storage you will need and the amount of ingredients necessary. Start with a small choice of ingredients and equipment and build up slowly rather than starting with everything available. This will make the first recipes much easier for the children to follow. St Peter's asked the children to get involved in labelling and making signs to support learning e.g. reminding the children to wash their hands, and labelling shelves. This gives the children ownership of the area, promotes writing and also saves time making laminated labels yourself. This also makes it easier to change as you introduce new recipes and ingredients.

As the recipes in this book become more focused on working together to create a group product rather than create an individual snack they include equipment and ingredients lists. This encourages children to look through the storage and check they have everything they need ready to begin.

"Keep it simple to start with and then build it up slowly."

Helen Hope, Owner, Norton Pre-School

"Shadow marking everything has really helped us and we have changed this depending on recipes or cohorts. We now shadow mark a basket or pot so that all you have to do is change the picture inside."

Stacey Hynd, EYFS lead, Thorley Hill Primary School

"Ensure you are providing adequate labelling for the ingredients and resources needed e.g. take photos of the actual items children will be using. Make sure there are not too many pieces of cooking equipment on show, start off giving the children what they need in the area and build up to them being able to make a more informed choice on the resources they may need."

Victoria Farrelly, EYFS lead, Trekenner Community Primary School

"Make it really clear on your recipes and your different size spoons which one is needed. Cling film, tin foil and sandwich bags come in handy for sending things home. Labels on greaseproof paper for when you are baking a batch of something works well."

Stacey Hynd, EYFS lead, Thorley Hill Primary School

"Having a choice of equipment available gives the children responsibility of selecting the tools they think will work effectively."

Alice Williams and Guy Barlow, Year One teachers, St Peter's Catholic Primary School

Opening and closing times

You need to decide whether your cooking area will be open all day or when it works for you. It might be that you only have use of the oven at certain times a day so certain recipes might be restricted. You need to be practical in terms of when the last group can start cooking so you are prepared at the end of the day.

"We had clear expectations of how the area was used with an open and closed sign."

Cassie Smith, EYFS Teacher, Decoy Community Primary School

Who can use the area?

There are some children who gravitate towards the cooking area every day, in the same way some would gravitate towards the water or art area. In most settings this wasn't an issue but if you want to monitor who is using the area and how often a simple sign-up sheet may be beneficial. It means that the children who haven't had a chance to cook that week have a fairer chance. All children should be accessing the provision. If you are asking for a termly contribution from parents, then this will be important to them too.

Examples

Here are some examples of set ups that might help to inspire you. Each area is different, but each has the following in common:

▶ Clearly defined area
▶ Storage/shelf space with clearly labelled containers or shelves. Places for equipment and ingredients
▶ Area for washing/drying up (nearby if possible)
▶ Clearly displayed recipes
▶ Space for children to prepare food
▶ Clearly displayed risk/benefit assessments

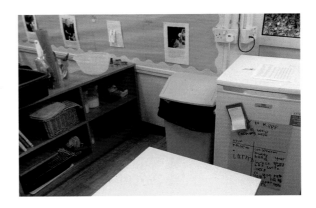

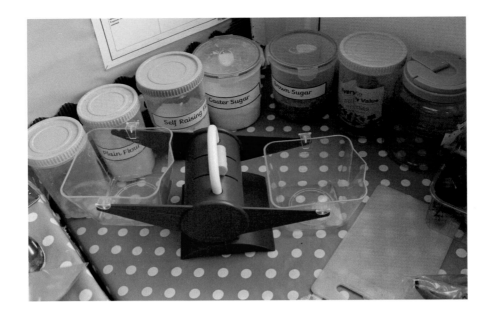

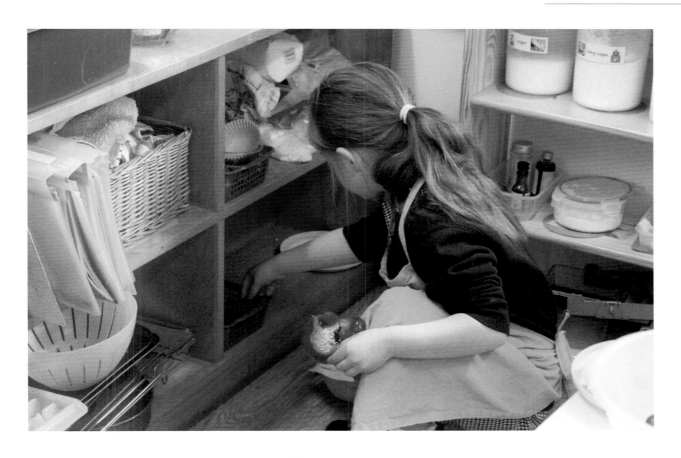

Displaying recipes

There are a few different ways you can store the recipes for the children to access. You might want to laminate and display the one you are using on the wall or you might want to create a collection for children to access as needed. Here are a few ways schools have approached this.

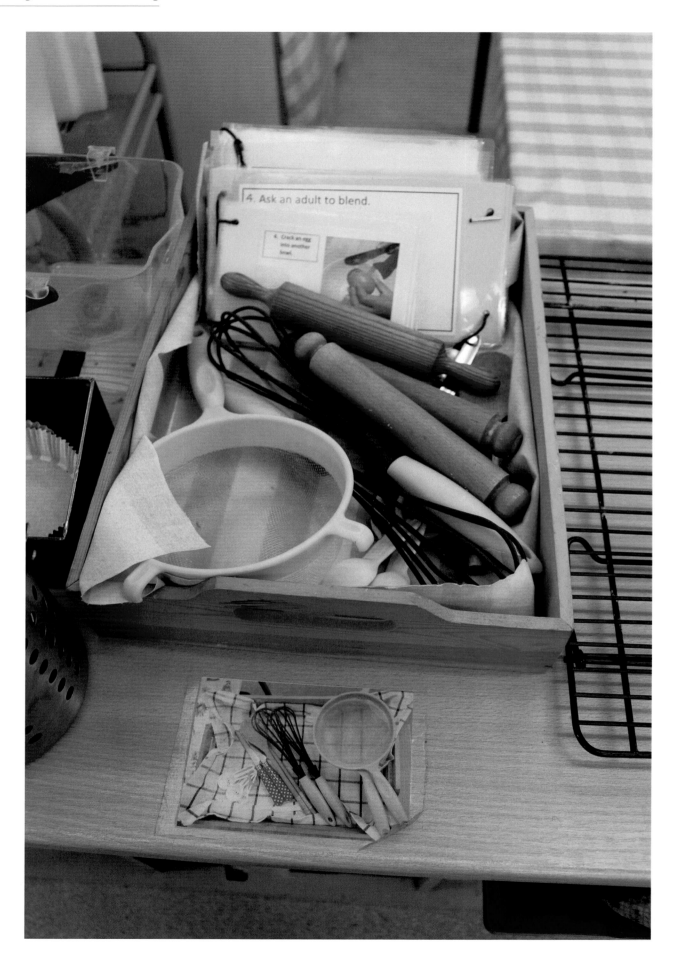

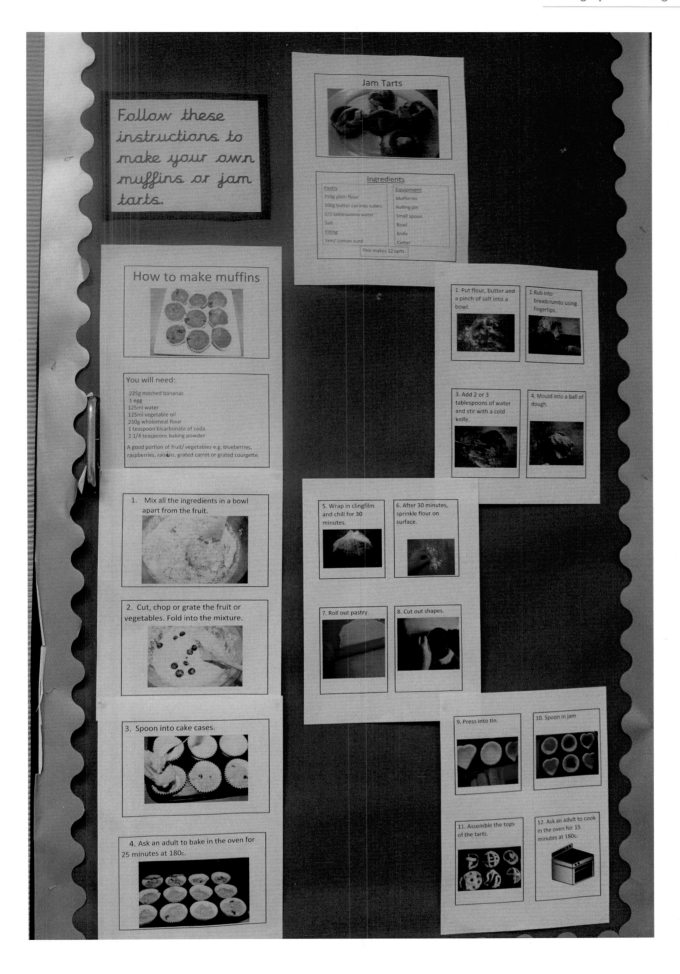

Follow these instructions to make your own muffins or jam tarts.

Jam Tarts

Ingredients

Pastry	Equipment
250g plain flour	Muffin tin
100g butter cut into cubes.	Rolling pin
2/3 tablespoons water	Small spoon
Salt	Bowl
Filling	Knife
Jam/ Lemon curd	Cutter

This makes 12 tarts.

How to make muffins

You will need:

225g mashed bananas
1 egg
125ml water
125ml vegetable oil
250g wholemeal flour
1 teaspoon bicarbonate of soda
2 1/4 teaspoons baking powder

A good portion of fruit/ vegetables e.g. blueberries, raspberries, raisins, grated carrot or grated courgette.

1. Mix all the ingredients in a bowl apart from the fruit.

2. Cut, chop or grate the fruit or vegetables. Fold into the mixture.

3. Spoon into cake cases.

4. Ask an adult to bake in the oven for 25 minutes at 180c.

1. Put flour, butter and a pinch of salt into a bowl.

2. Rub into breadcrumbs using fingertips.

3. Add 2 or 3 tablespoons of water and stir with a cold knife.

4. Mould into a ball of dough.

5. Wrap in clingfilm and chill for 30 minutes.

6. After 30 minutes, sprinkle flour on surface.

7. Roll out pastry.

8. Cut out shapes.

9. Press into tin.

10. Spoon in jam

11. Assemble the tops of the tarts.

12. Ask an adult to cook in the oven for 15 minutes at 180c.

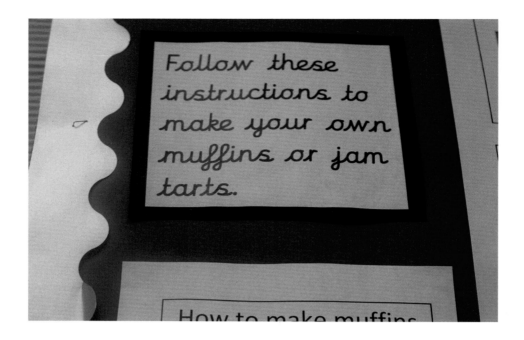

Visitors

Although you may be confident in your belief that cooking will benefit children and allow them to learn across the curriculum, it may be helpful to share this knowledge and understanding with others. That way there can be no doubt that this area of learning is effective and relevant. Here are a couple of ways that you can do this if you wish.

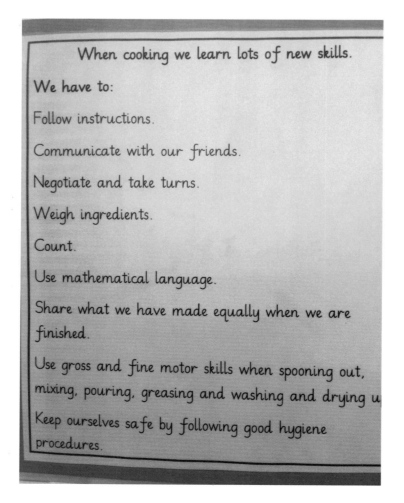

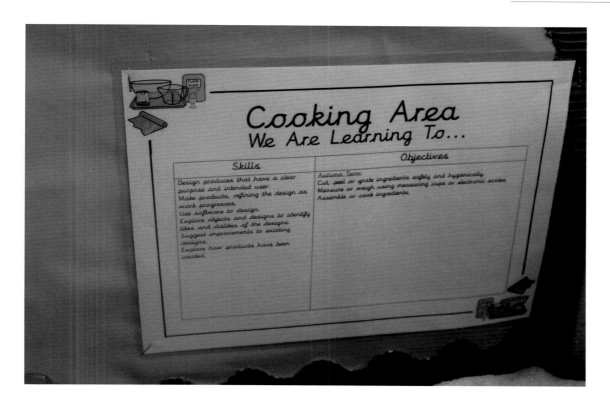

However you choose to set up your areas, as with any area of provision it will evolve, as the children do, throughout the year. No one cooking or snack area will look the same and it is important to create an environment which works for your own setting.

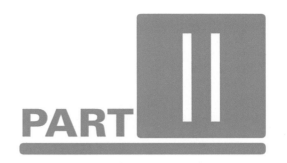

PART II

Recipes and guidance

Early Years Foundation Stage – recipes

Fruit salad
Salad
Fruit faces
Salad pot
Fruit kebabs
Salad kebabs
Rice cake snacks
Cucumber and celery bites
Orange juice
Lemonade
Smoothies
Fruit milkshakes
Yoghurt bites
Porridge
Yoghurt lollies
Fruit lollies
Pancakes
Chocolate nests
Potato salad
Pasta salad
Jam tarts
Cheese and tomato bites
Bagel pizza
Fruit pies
Garlic bread
Banana, strawberry and yoghurt smoothie
Vegetable soup
Cake
Biscuits
Bread

Key Stage One – recipes

Sandwiches/wraps
Vegetable tarts
Smoothies
Leek and potato soup
Banana loaf
Carrot cake
Flapjacks
Fruit crumble
Gingerbread
Bread
Muffins
Scones
Cheese straws
Hot cross buns
Pancakes
Falafel burgers or balls
Quiche
Pizza
Jam or lemon tarts
Book of dips

CHAPTER 7

EYFS recipe guidance

Introduction

The recipes in this section are aimed at children working within the EYFS curriculum. They are specifically aimed towards 3- to 5-year-olds. The recipes begin with simple suggestions for preparing fruit and salad in different ways. This will give the children the opportunity to use equipment and to learn some of the skills involved in food preparation. They are designed to be quick, simple, snack preparation recipes that children and teachers/practitioners can use to encourage the children to explore a variety of healthy snack options. These recipes can, of course been used with older children as the outcome will be very different.

As the recipes progress they become more involved, needing the children to find equipment and ingredients and work through a recipe. These recipes are aimed really at Reception-aged children. Teachers and practitioners however are free to use any recipe from any section depending on the skills and experience of the children as well as the level of adult support. Many of these recipes will be suitable for Key Stage One as the children will still benefit from the skills they involve.

In this chapter, there is a brief description of the recipes and the type of learning experience each encourages. There are also some tips on how to approach the recipes and what might enhance them. The children will bring their own uniqueness to the recipes and the outcomes will very much depend on them, making each cooking/food session preparation unique. The possibilities are indeed endless.

Fruit salad and salad

These simple, easy to follow recipe cards are perfect for allowing the children to explore healthy foods, tastes and textures. You may need to talk to the children first about portion size and decide what your own expectations are. Are they making individual portions to eat on the snack table? Are they making a group dish to share or are they making a snack for the whole class to access in the snack area?

These recipes encourage children to be creative. They may want to design their dish first or just go for it. Each year group can approach these recipes differently and you can adjust the level of challenge to suit your class.

"I modelled the knife skills for the chopping, talking about safety and there were levels of difficulty, banana leading to pineapple which was more of a challenge. We discussed healthy foods as they worked. I encouraged them to make their own recipe card to display and show others how to make it – lots of representing number and mark making. To extend for the 40–60 m children I suggested they instead (or as well as) think of their own fruit salad recipe to make for next time (which they did!)."

Louisa Cowler, Owner and Manager, Sunflowers Pre-School

The children at Thorley Hill decided to make a large salad to share.

"The fruit salad was so easy for them to access independently and they loved it! The different designs they are naturally coming up with are fantastic. The children have been making them and then sharing them around the class as well as at the snack table so they are really thinking about their portion size and presentation. I now have a little shopping list that they have written for me with different suggestions of things they have in their salads at home or things they would like to try. The washing up is so easy as well which appeals to them. I added in a grater as well as the knife which they are using in all sorts of interesting ways. We go over the health and safety rules first but then they are off. Lots of mathematical talk about sharing ingredients and how to divide it up evenly, shape (cutting into cubes, cuboids, pyramids, squares, circles, diamonds etc). Great vocab slices, diced, chunks. . . . Describing the taste juicy, crunchy, wet, fresh, green, sweet etc. The talk about healthy foods, healthy teeth and where our food goes. The list goes on. Give this one a go if you can. So much you could do with Year 1 and 2 especially regarding design, orders, and healthy eating."

Stacey Hynd, EYFS lead, Thorley Hill Primary School

"I like the salad best because it was yummy! It had tomatoes and green stuff."

Reception child

"It is healthy because it is fruit and vegetables."

Reception child

Trekenner decided to use the fruit salad as a way of introducing a snack café. One group prepared a large fruit salad and then the children came to buy their fruit at snack time. The teacher added yoghurt to the menu and used this as an opportunity for the children to practise using money, adding amounts in a real-life context.

"The children have all benefited in a variety of ways from using our snack cafe daily. The consistency allows children to practise basic number skills using real money. They find the quickest ways to pay e.g. taking 2p away to keep and giving 8p to the cashier. Children with EAL and Speech and Language needs can develop their confidence in acquiring new or familiar vocabulary in a relaxed and contextual manner.

We often put out new fruit like grapefruit and kiwi to encourage the children to try new foods. We find they are much more likely to try it if they have prepared it rather than having it put out for them."

Victoria Farrelly, EYFS lead, Trekenner Community Primary School

Ashleigh Primary School made a salad bar with prices for children to prepare their own salad, paying for it at the end. The children worked independently to make their own salad, often creating a design or picture. Some children were able to work out the payment independently and recorded this on a whiteboard and if not, the adults used this as a teachable moment.

Year One at St Peters used the fruit salad to teach fractions with each child selecting a piece of fruit and cutting it into quarters to share with the group. When observing the children, they had a detailed discussion about which fruit each child would select with some children trying to persuade other children to choose a fruit they all liked. The teachers had labelled each packet of fruit, so the children knew what a portion was e.g. eight blueberries which would then need to be shared between four. They provided the children with a little juice to add at the end if they liked. Some of the children made their own juice by squeezing their orange segment over the fruit rather than adding the juice.

"I don't like orange juice but I like orange juice from oranges when I squeeze them." Year One child

Fruit faces, salad pot, fruit kebabs, salad kebabs, rice cake snacks, cucumber and celery bites

These recipes make individual portions and are particularly suitable for EYFS. They are designed to be independent so can be left in the snack area for children to access then enjoy straight away. Children could use the I-Pads/cameras to take a picture of their creation and add to the cooking working wall to give their peers ideas.

Fruit faces

"They had practiced knife safety and chopping so I decided to lead them into talking about shape and noticing detailed features. I made a face with all the fruit available to show them different possibilities and demonstrated a few different ways to cut the grapes and banana to make it look like different things, e.g. end of the banana for a nose. I encouraged them to have a plan in mind as they chopped the fruit and most of them started and adapted as they went along, changing their mind as they discovered a new shape to cut! The children did comment on circles, triangles etc and I was honestly shocked at how completely different and unique every one was – I thought there would be a few that followed the other but they all had their own ideas which was great as it led us on to looking at each other and how all of their faces were different and unique! Some described their faces as 'grumpy/happy' and I quoted them on how they tasted and what they liked about them soon after they had eaten to add to their photos! I can set this up in the snack area now it's been modelled once and the children will independently access it! They are very confident with this."

Louisa Cowler, Owner and Manager, Sunflowers Pre-School

Salad pots

A simple idea for children to prepare their own mini salad pot. This recipe could easily be replicated with fruit to create fruit pots instead. Once they are confident chopping, pots can be left on the table for them to make their own snack.

Thorley Hill found that maths naturally came into the salad pot with children counting how many pieces they had of each item and either sharing them between them or checking there would be enough left for their peers. The children halved the tomatoes and were using the language of sharing naturally.

"I'm going to use half of this tomato. Would you like the other half?"

Reception child

Fruit kebabs and salad kebabs

This is a great recipe for allowing children to naturally explore pattern. Each child wanted to fill up their kebab and was very particular about what they put on and in which order. As the kebab sticks were a little sharp at the end (the wooden ones presented less of a risk) you may need to spend time talking about safety, always pointing the stick down and never towards faces and eyes!

Rice cake snacks

This is a simple recipe perfect for Pre-School and Nursery. The children add cream cheese to their faces and then use their chopping skills to add fruit/salad.

"What's those green bits?" Nursery child

"You need to cut it in half." Nursery child

"It's like putting butter on toast" Nursery child

The children at Thorley Hill Nursery made Rice Cake Faces. The teacher washed the fruit with the children the first time and reminded them how to chop the fruit safely. They spent time exploring shape, space and measure as they carefully cut each piece to size. They used appropriate shapes and used the language of shape and size throughout. The teacher used the opportunity to introduce or reinforce names of the fruit and talked about seeds, encouraging the children to consider where the fruit came from.

When the children were eating their rice cakes a practitioner stopped to ask them about their creations and used it as an opportunity to talk about shape and properties, focussing on circles. Talking about shape in this real context really encouraged the children to consider shapes as part of their world and the following day some of the children spotted circles in their environment and came to tell the practitioner what they had seen.

"The rice cake recipe was a great way to introduce the use of knives and developing their independence. I was surprised by how well they managed and how little support they needed to prepare their own snack."

Louise da Costa, Nursery Teacher, Thorley Hill Primary School

101

Cucumber and celery bites

This recipe is a nice starting point for the children to create using cucumber as a base. At Ashleigh Primary School, once the children had followed the recipe, they became more experimental, using the ingredients they liked the most. You could add more ingredients such as sweetcorn and mini peppers for children to experiment further with textures and tastes.

Ashleigh had a rule that the children had to eat or at least try what they had made so this made the children very selective. The portion size was perfect as a snack with the children making two each.

Orange juice and lemonade

So many cooking experiences are fantastic for whole hand development. Making these juices means that the children are twisting, pushing and grinding to get the most out of their fruit. It is interesting to see how much strength and stamina different children show whilst using the juicer.

It can be messy but the children loved tasting their own juices. They can try the pure juice they have made or add a jug of water so the children could make their juice go a bit further, diluting it slightly.

Lemonade works in a very similar way but this recipe encourages children to sweeten to taste. Whilst this may not seem like the healthiest option it does promote a lot of talk about how much sugar is needed to make it sweet enough to resemble some of the children's own drinks. Thorley Hill made lemonade to share with their families at their end of year celebration.

Smoothies, fruit milkshakes, yoghurt bites, porridge, yoghurt lollies, fruit lollies, pancakes, chocolate nests

These recipes are all simple to follow but will need an adult to either cook, bake or blend or freeze them at some point during the process.

Smoothies and fruit milkshakes

Smoothies and fruit milkshakes are fantastic open-ended recipes which encourage the tasting of new fruits and vegetables, but the children do make them quite quickly so an adult has to be on hand to blend. The children could put theirs in named pots to blend at the end of the morning. This one is good for looking at capacity and volume with the children. How full does the pot need to be? How much liquid do you think we need?

The children in St Michael's Nursery made strawberry milkshakes using freshly picked strawberries from their garden.

Yoghurt bites

Quick, easy and adaptable. You can try many different fruits and yoghurts for this recipe.

Porridge

Like pancakes, this one is quick so the children could make theirs with an adult or leave the batches to cook later. They could write their names next to their bowl to save.

You could add fruit toppings for the children to try, make a special porridge for Goldilocks or re-create the three bears' different tastes.

Yoghurt and fruit lollies

In a similar way to the salad bar, a lolly station can be set up. This is a great way for children to try different fruits. The children could work in pairs to make a combination together or work as a group to make a few lollies for the class. They will need an adult present to blend their fruit but could leave it in pots with their names on for later preparation if you want to have a blending session later in the day, perhaps before home time. The children could blend all their fruit or leave little chunks to add to their mix after it has been blended to create different textures.

This is a fantastic recipe for children to compare to shop-purchased products. They could make a list of their own ingredients and compare this to the information on the packaging. This would be particularly suitable for Key Stage One.

Pancakes

A very quick recipe so be prepared to have an adult on hand to fry the pancakes with the children or ask the children to make their own batch to be made later. There are three recipes to choose from. The simplest is in cups and the next two recipes are good for counting. You can choose from the smaller and larger mix version. The milk could either be premeasured or a line could be drawn on the jug to show the children where the milk should reach. Whisking might be a new skill for the children and they often end up working in pairs with one whisking and one holding the bowl, demonstrating great problem solving and teamwork. The children loved trying the different toppings on offer with the pancakes.

"We gave the children the responsibility to decide whether they were cool enough to eat. You can use the toppings to talk about patterns, and they could cut their own toppings as well."

Kelli Stocker, EYFS lead, St Michael's Church of England (VA) Primary School

Chocolate nests

A treat recipe perfect for Easter!

Potato salad, pasta salad, jam tarts, cheese and tomato bites, bagel pizza, fruit pies, garlic bread, banana, strawberry and yoghurt smoothie, vegetable soup

These recipes have more of an involved process with specific instructions. They require the children to follow instructions, work as a group and remained focussed on the activity for a sustained period of time. As the cooking is purposeful and the children have chosen to do it this is rarely a problem. The children take their time working through the instructions, chatting to each other, negotiating turn taking and spending time exploring the ingredients. These recipes begin to ask the children to find their own ingredients and equipment before starting which schools found a useful tool for helping children to get themselves organised.

Potato salad and pasta salad

These recipes come in two forms so you can choose how you would like to approach this. The children can either follow the recipe in a group to make a group salad portion or you could leave the ingredients for the children to explore and make their own pasta/potato salad. The children could follow the recipe to begin with then use the more open-ended one as a follow up. We tended to open the tins for the children making sure that the tin edges were no longer sharp but you could equally ask the children to open the tins if you felt they were competent and it was safe.

Jam tarts

A recipe for a treat. Some schools used these for Valentine's day and Mother's day but you can use them whenever you like. An easy to follow recipe for the children, allowing for lots of independence.

Cheese and tomato bites

Sunflowers Pre-School made cheese and tomato bites. They modelled it with each child then left the ingredients out in the provision for the children to make themselves to be baked at the end of the day. Sunflowers decided to use metal cutters as they were easier to cut through the wrap.

"The children shared a chopping board, cutters and then a tray – they had to count and work out how many cheese and tomato bites they would have each. They managed to push the shapes into the cupcake tray holes completely independently.

I let the children judge how big a spoonful of passata they would need to put at the bottom and modelled how to do a 'sprinkle' of cheese on top. I asked them to predict what we were going to do next and how the oven would change the cheese. Lots of discussion of texture and new words discovered! We ran out of time so a lot of the children actually took theirs home. One parent enjoyed them so much we had a request for the recipe and instructions and she sent us in an observation on tapestry of how they looked! They were fab!"

Louisa Cowler, Owner and Manager, Sunflowers Pre-School

Bagel pizza

This recipe is fantastic for exploring different pizza toppings and vegetables. This a great opportunity for children to try food like peppers and fresh tomato. The children from Reception in St Michael's worked calmly and sensibly, all the time talking about what they were doing, explaining their opinions and choices. They shared equipment and took turns with the ingredients. They supported each other's choices, helped each other to use equipment by demonstrating e.g. how to use the grater. Each bagel looked different before cooking with the children making their own unique pizza.

St Michael's Nursery made pizza on bases as an adaption, using vegetables and herbs from their garden. You could also use a baguette cut in half which works well.

Fruit pies

This recipe involves halves of fruits and spices so this is a good teaching opportunity for teaching halving. It also involves counting to 15 and lots of physical skills such as cutting pastry, using a small spoon and squeezing a lemon.

Garlic bread

Once the children are familiar with the toaster they could use this recipe to make their own garlic bread and cheesy garlic bread. You can use any type of bread for this ranging from ciabatta to sliced bread – just make sure it fits in the toaster.

Banana, strawberry and yoghurt smoothie

A simple smoothie recipe that involves counting.

Vegetable soup

A soup maker is perfect for making soup with the children if you want them to chop and prepare the vegetables. You could either cook and then try the soups as a class or take it home for dinner.

Thorley Hill asked each child to keep named Tupperware at school for their cooking which worked perfectly for soup. St Michael's children took their soup home in zip bags.

If you were making a class soup the children could each contribute a vegetable and then share out the soup. When using the soup maker, the children can be involved in estimating how much water they should use. The soup maker should take around 20 minutes to cook so the children could time this using stopwatches or tablets. They can get hot when cooking so remember to plug the soup maker in away from the children and use with supervision.

Baking recipes – cake, bread, biscuits

The baking recipes all involve mixing ingredients so are great for exploring textures and smells. The children can really get stuck into mixing and kneading which is fantastic for developing strength and stamina. When using the butter ensure it is soft enough for the children to be able to mix. It can become frustrating if the butter is too hard so either softened butter or cooking margarine work well. These recipes are specific in their measurements and the children need to follow them closely.

"We had the laminated cards on the wall showing the sequence the children needed to go through to make their cakes. The first picture shows someone washing their hands and wearing an apron. The last picture shows them they need to wash up their equipment when they have finished."

Louise da Costa, Nursery Teacher, Thorley Hill Primary School

Cake is a fantastic way of allowing the children to become familiar with the concept of weighing and balancing. The children pick up the language very quickly and are soon naturally using this language with each other.

"No that's not balanced. You need to take some out because that one is too heavy."

Reception child

The cake can be decorated so give the children further opportunity to be creative. Once they have been shown how to make simple icing with icing sugar and water they can use small quantities to decorate their large cake or their cupcakes. This has been a real favourite with lots of children who have loved exploring different decorations. The small sprinkles and items are perfect for developing fine motor skills and require good hand-eye coordination.

"My favourite thing is to cook is cupcakes and I like adding the sprinkles."

Reception child

Once the children have become accomplished at this they often find occasions that need a cake! It might be their birthday or the birthday member of a staff. They love surprising their friends and family with this thoughtful gesture and often need very little encouragement to include a note or card with the cake. This creates a real purpose for writing and such enthusiasm.

On one occasion we saw a child explain to their friends he would like to make a birthday cake for his brother and his two friends quickly agreed they wanted to help, asking the teacher if they could do this. The teacher explained that if they made one big cake the two friends would not be able to take any home and they didn't hesitate to assure the teacher that they didn't mind.

One of the children at Thorley Hill surprised them by adding butter to her icing mix and simply explained "I wanted butter icing instead." This led to children exploring textures of icing and adding cocoa to make it chocolate icing.

Cake is fantastic for introducing fractions to young children in context. They very quickly pick up that a large cake needs to be shared equally and develop an understanding of halves, thirds and quarters. Thorley Hill use this as teachable moment and often ask the children to divide the cake up at the end of the day in front of the class so they all become familiar with the concept.

Ashleigh often did this, then asked the children to think about who they were going to share their cake with at home and divide up their own piece into the relevant number of pieces.

Cupcakes, biscuits and bread are also great for sharing. The children often naturally count how many they have made altogether and want to work out how many they will take home, so they can be heard discussing this throughout. They know it has to be fair and it is interesting to see how they deal with a left-over cake! This can be another opportunity for gifting a cake with a little card. They often travel all over schools, sometimes to the office staff and sometimes as thank you to the caretaker.

With these baking recipes, the products are often taken home so most settings left reusable sealable bags named for each child. Some settings asked the children to write their names on a blank sticker and put it on the bag as a way of reinforcing name writing. Others asked them to put their name on a small piece of card and put it inside the bag so the bags could be returned and reused.

These recipes often involve quite a few ingredients so the children need to be familiar with the set up for getting out and putting away. Clearly labelled shelves help with this and once the expectations have been set for a tidy working table then most children become good at putting away each ingredient as they have finished with them.

When baking with these recipes, children are becoming familiar with standard measure and the importance of accuracy with measure. They can demonstrate great skill with this. Once they have been taught to level off tablespoons and teaspoons they remember this and remind each other frequently.

These recipes use teaspoons and tablespoons so remember to highlight the difference between these before beginning. This can lead to lots of discussions using the language of size between the children.

"The tablespoon is the biggest one and the teaspoon is smaller."

Reception child

These recipes involve lots of physical skills such as mixing, rolling, kneading, pouring, cutting, mashing.

As the children become more confident they often ask to experiment and adapt the recipes. This might need some planning in order to check you have the ingredients they need e.g. raisins or chocolate chips for cakes, lemon for biscuits or you might feel that you want to put out a few extra choices for them to experiment with.

CHAPTER 8

Key Stage One recipe guidance

Introduction

These recipes in Key Stage One all have different skills. Some involve more of a design element, some encourage exploration of new foods, and some require children to use their knowledge of standard measure. They each require different amounts of time. It is important to select according to the needs and interests of your children.

Children in Key Stage One, especially Year One, will still benefit from many EYFS recipes so feel free to select recipes from the EYFS section. Particularly useful from this section may be the more open-ended recipes like salads and soups but also the recipes involving counting if they are not yet confident with standard measure.

> "They loved making smoothies as it was totally independent, and we always had the ingredients to hand in school so free too!"
>
> Penny Hopkinson, Year Two teacher, St Michael's C of E (VA) Primary School
>
> "Soup was good for practising cutting techniques for different vegetables and their motor skill development. We asked them to think about which vegetables went together. The children were excited to take their soups home to share with their family."
>
> Rachel Griffiths, Assistant Head, Year One teacher, St Michael's C of E (VA) Primary School

As discussed in the Key Stage One curriculum chapter it is easy to add challenge to these recipes by asking them to design, make and evaluate as they cook or giving them a specific maths or curricular focus. The following guidance should help you to select appropriate recipes.

Sandwiches, wraps, vegetable tarts and smoothies

These recipes don't require the children to measure but do need them to estimate how much filling, fruit, vegetables and water they need. They require teamwork and the children will have to explain their thinking and justify their ideas to others if they are making something together. They also give the children the chance to practise their cutting skills and food preparation skills.

Perhaps with the sandwiches they could take orders for a lunchtime shop or work to make one for their friends instead of themselves. Thorley Hill made alternative sandwiches for Paddington Bear when the children took an interest in the film.

Children could make a menu of sandwiches or even run their own café. Computing could be used throughout the process for the children to take photos of their product, following this by writing instructions and displaying for others. The children have so many ideas of what they would like to make. By providing an environment where they can lead their own learning the possibilities for cross-curricular learning is endless.

Leek and potato soup

Here is a specific recipe for the children to follow. It might give them more ideas to design their own soup again. Peeling a potato will be a new skill for most of the children so they will need to be shown this in order to peel it safely.

Banana loaf and carrot cake

These recipes use amounts up to and under 100 g. The processes are quite simple, but you could, as always, allow the children to add their own ideas. What could we make instead of carrot cake but using the same recipe? Can we add any extras to the banana loaf, would it make any difference? Encouraging the children to use the recipes as a basis for cooking and allowing them to add their own ideas is so beneficial as the children are seeing themselves as inventors and learners whilst practising the skills that cooking enables.

"The children were very clear about what they wanted to achieve. They were able to suggest alternative ingredients and ask about what ingredients worked well with the others and which did not. They have suggested recipes we could make as a class."

Vittoria Townsend, Year Two teacher, Thorley Hill Primary School

Flapjacks and fruit crumble

These recipes have an easy to follow process but are still open to experimentation. What fruit could the children add to the crumble? Schools might grow their own apples, blackberries or rhubarb for the children to use.

Gingerbread

There are quite a lot of ingredients in this recipe and it will take children a while to make and shape the dough. It is a lovely Christmas recipe.

Bread

Making bread involves the children using standard measure, including ML. This is another great recipe for being inventive and thinking about ingredients. The children can add anything they like to the bread. St. Michael's used herbs from their garden and Thorley Hill used a variety of seeds and fruits. When they are preparing the bread they will need time for it to rise.

As the recipes continue they encourage the children to be less reliant on photos as prompts and therefore rely on children using their comprehension skills. This will promote a lot of discussion as children read the recipes aloud and discuss what each step means.

Muffins and scones

These are great for experimenting with ingredients and dividing mixtures. The children can be very adventurous with their additions both savoury and sweet.

"We asked the children to add different fruit to their muffins (bananas, blueberries, carrot etc). It was a great lesson in compromise – deciding on an addition that everyone wanted. One group managed to divide their mixture up so that each person got what they wanted. Some great Maths!"

Alice Williams and Guy Barlow, Year One teachers, St Peter's Catholic Primary School

Cheese straws

The cheese straws are a good recipe for letting the children make their own designs.

"The children measured the ingredients but then adapted them to their liking. They made different shapes and used different amounts of cheese each time."

Holly Skinner, Key Stage One lead, St Peter's Catholic Primary School

Hot cross buns

A handy recipe for Easter time.

"Hot cross buns were so easy and looked amazing!"

Penny Hopkinson, Year Two teacher, St Michael's C of E (VA) Primary School

Pancakes and falafel burgers or balls

These recipes will need an adult to fry at the end of cooking. Pancakes are simple and quick where falafel takes longer. Falafel involves chopping onion so children will need to be shown this either whilst cooking or prior to cooking. There are quite a few spices in this recipe so it is a nice one for thinking about smells.

Quiche, pizza, jam or lemon tarts

For these recipes the children will be making the pastry so bear in mind they will need time to do this. It is a nice move from the previous recipes where the children have previously used shop-bought pastry or bases and gives them a good chance to get really see the whole cooking process.

The pizzas, for example, are a step up from the children making bagel pizzas in EYFS and perhaps Year One. St Peter's used pizzas to teach fractions, asking the children to plan portions. In some cases the children agreed what would be on their pizza and in other groups children divided the pizza into thirds or quarters with different toppings.

Book of dips

The dip recipes can be made into a little book for children to use as they wish. They might choose one to make or each new group could make one to try. All of the dips apart from hummus don't require any measure. The children will need to estimate how much they need to add of each ingredient. You could use a book of all of them or just choose a few at a time. The hummus recipe is great for fractions. These recipes are physical with lots of mashing, grinding, squeezing and tearing.

These dips are great for the children to make for sharing for a social snack time or for celebration or open evenings to share with families and visitors.

These recipes will give children in Key Stage One time to develop basic cooking skills and learn across the curriculum whilst continuing to promote active learning and the Characteristics of Effective Learning.

EYFS recipes

Fruit salad

1 Select your fruit.

2 Wash, prepare and chop your fruit.

3 Arrange your fruit.

Salad

1 Select your salad.

2 Wash, prepare and chop your salad.

3 Arrange your salad.

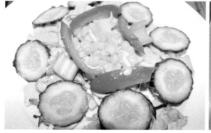  

Fruit faces

1 Wash the fruit.

2 Cut the fruit.

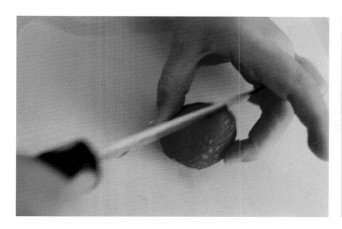 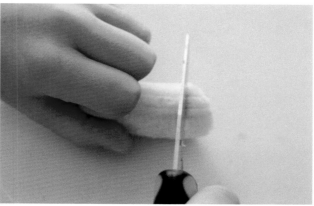

3 Make a face.

129

Salad pot

1 Wash the salad.

2 Chop or cut the salad.

3 Put in pot.

Fruit kebabs

1 Wash the fruit.

2 Cut the fruit.

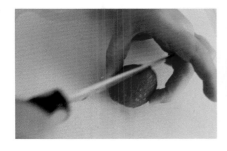 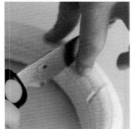

3 Thread onto sticks.

Salad kebabs

1 Wash the salad.

2 Cut or chop the salad.

3 Thread onto sticks.

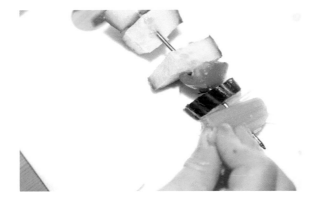

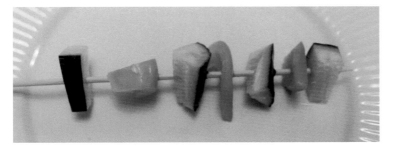

Rice cake snacks

1 Put rice cake on a plate.

2 Spread on soft cheese or butter.

3 Wash and chop fruit or vegetables.

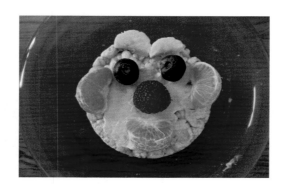

4 Arrange toppings.

Cucumber and celery bites

1 Wash and cut cucumber and celery.

2 Spoon soft cheese into celery and onto cucumber.

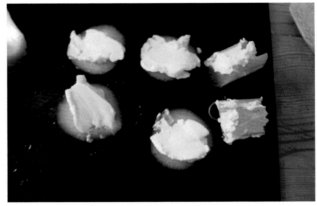

3 Wash, chop tomatoes or peel and grate carrot.

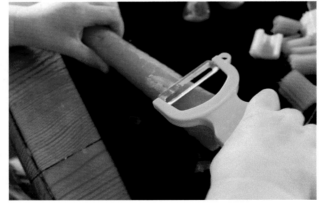

4   Add tomato or carrot toppings.

Orange juice

1 Cut the orange in half.

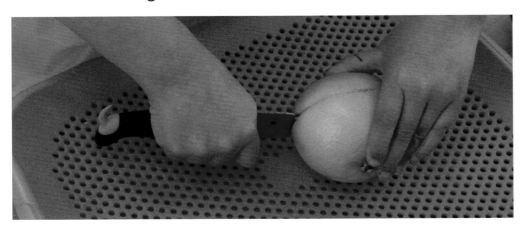

2 Squeeze the orange.

3 Pour into a glass.

4 Add the pulp if you like it.

5 Drink.

Lemonade

1 Cut lemon in half.

2 Squeeze lemon.

3 Pour into a glass.

4 Add water.

5 Add sugar.

6 Stir.

Smoothies

1 Wash the fruit and vegetables.

2 Cut the fruit and vegetables.

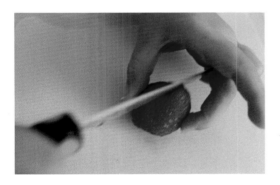 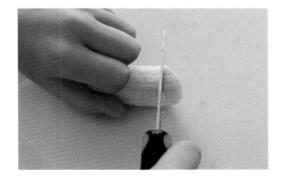

3 Put in jug and add water.

4 Ask an adult to blend.

5 Pour.

Fruit milkshakes

1 Wash the fruit.

2 Cut the fruit.

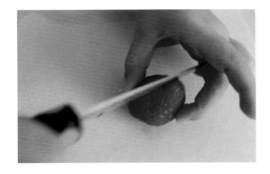

3 Put in the jug and add milk.

4 Ask an adult to blend.

5 Pour.

Yoghurt bites

1 Spoon in yoghurt.

2 Wash and cut fruit.

 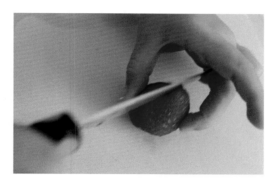

3 Add fruit.

4 Freeze.

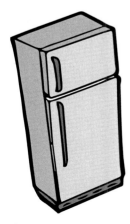

Porridge

1 Add 1 cup water.

2 Add 2 cups milk.

3 Add 1 cup oats.

4 Mix.

5 Ask an adult to microwave.

Yoghurt lollies

You will need

Fruit

Yoghurt

Mortar and pestle

Colander

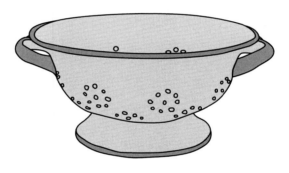

A freezer

Lolly moulds

Spoon

What to do

1 Wash and crush fruit.

2 Add yoghurt.

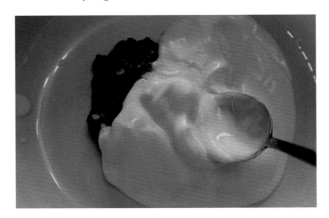

3 Mix.

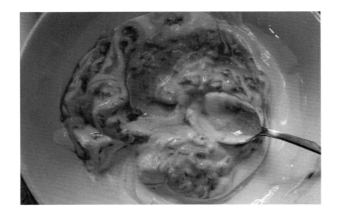

4 Put in lolly moulds.

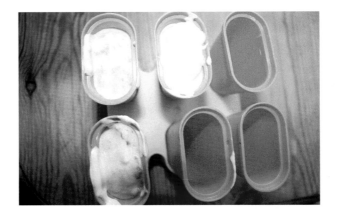

5 Freeze.

Fruit lollies

You will need

Fruit

Lolly moulds

Colander

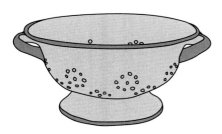

A freezer

Knife

Blender

Spoon

Chopping board

What to do

1 Wash fruit.

2 Chop fruit.

3 Ask an adult to blend fruit.

4 Put in lolly moulds.

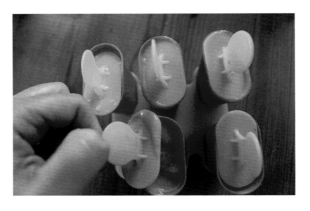

5 Freeze.

Pancakes

Ingredients

Flour
Egg
Milk
Toppings

What you need

Whisk

Bowl

Frying Pan

Tablespoon

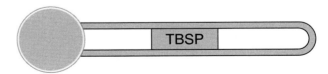

What to do

1 Put 6 tbsp. flour in a bowl.

2 Add 1 egg.

3 Add 16 tbsp. of milk.

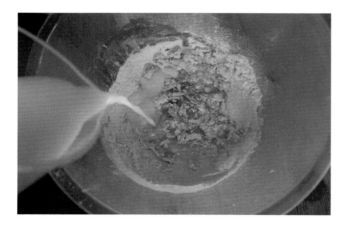

4 Whisk the ingredients together.

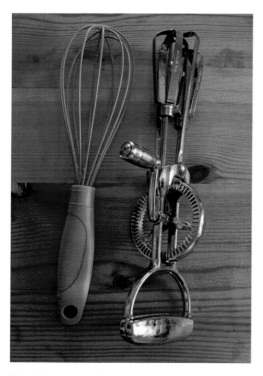

5 Ask an adult to fry the pancake.

6 Choose your toppings.

7 Fill and roll your pancake.

 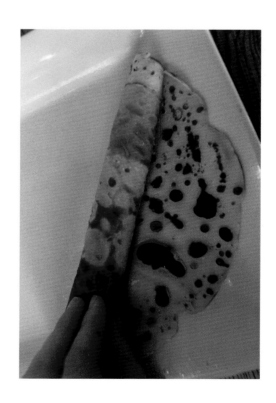

Chocolate nests

Ingredients

Chocolate (16 squares)
2 Shredded wheat
8 chocolate eggs are needed to make 4 nests.

What you need

Bowl

Small spoon

Cake cases

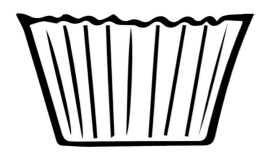

What to do

1 Crush 2 shredded wheat.

2 Ask an adult to melt the chocolate.

3 Mix.

4 Spoon into cases.

5 Add eggs.

Potato salad

Ingredients

Potato

Mayonnaise

Sour cream

Salad

Chives

What you need

Knife

Scissors

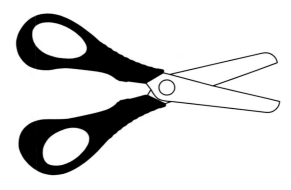

Bowl

Colander

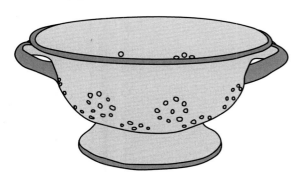

Chopping board

Mixing spoon

Large spoon

What to do

1 Chop potatoes.

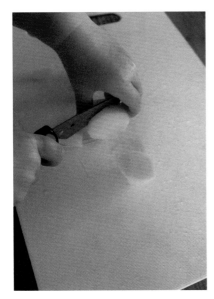

2 Wash, chop and add the salad.

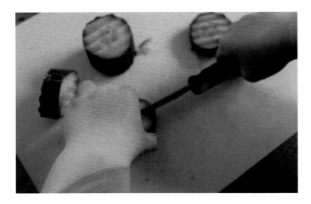

3 Add 1 large spoon mayonnaise.

4 Add 2 large spoons sour cream.

5 Cut some chives.

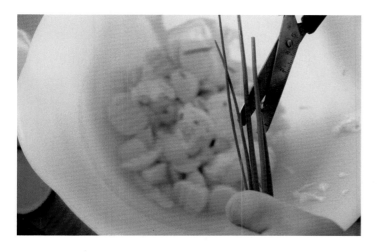

6 Mix.

Potato or pasta salad

Add potato or pasta.

Add salad.

Add mayonnaise or leave plain.

Jam tarts

Ingredients

Flour
Shortcrust pastry
Jam/lemon curd

What you need

Rolling pin

Small spoon

Muffin tray

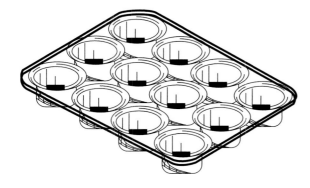

Cutters

Remember to ask an adult to turn the oven on.

What to do

1 Sprinkle flour.

2 Roll out pastry.

3 Cut shapes.

4 Press into tray.

5 Spoon in jam.

6 Ask an adult to cook in the oven for 15 minutes at 180°C.

Cheese and tomato bites

Ingredients

1 wrap

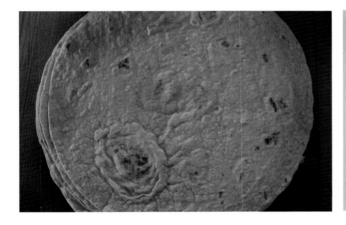

Passata

Cheese

What you need

Cutters

Small spoon

Grater

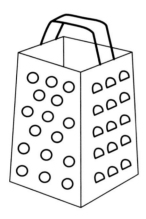

Muffin tray

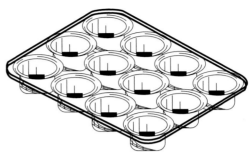

Remember to ask an adult to turn the oven on.

What to do

1   Grate the cheese.

2   Cut wrap into circles.

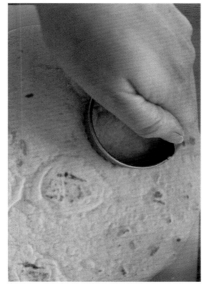

3   Press circles into tray.

4   Spoon passata into wraps.

5   Sprinkle cheese on the top.

6   Ask an adult to put in the oven for 10 minutes at 180°C.

Bagel pizza

Ingredients

Bagel

Passata

Cheese

Toppings

What you need

Spoon

Grater

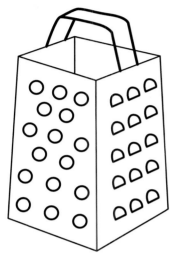

Baking tray

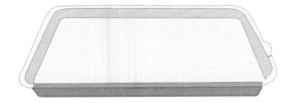

Chopping board

Knife

What to do

1 Cut the bagels in half.

2 Spread sauce over bagels.

3 Grate cheese and sprinkle over the top.

4 Wash, chop and add vegetables to the top.

5 Ask an adult to grill for 15 minutes.

Fruit pies

Ingredients

15 raspberries
½ apple
1 pear
½ lemon
Brown sugar
Shortcrust pastry
Cinnamon

What you need

Knife

Cutter

Rolling pin

Chopping board

Spoon

Muffin tray

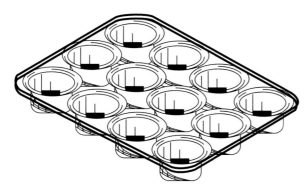

Bowl

Teaspoon

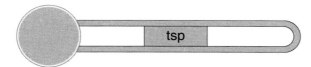

Remember to ask an adult to turn the oven on.

What to do

1 Roll the pastry and cut out circles. Press into tray.

2 Chop fruit and put in bowl.

3 Add 3 tsp. sugar.   4 Add ½ tsp. cinnamon.

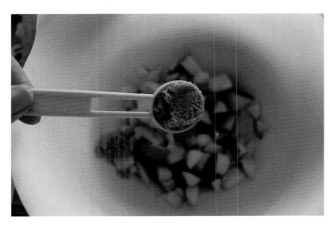 

5 Squeeze lemon into bowl.

6 Mix.

7 Spoon fruit mixture into cases.

8 Cut smaller circles and put on top. Press edges together to seal.

9 Make a cross and small hole on the top.

10 Ask an adult to put in the oven for 10 minutes at 180°C.

Garlic bread

Ingredients

Butter
Bread
Parsley
Olive oil
Garlic
A pinch of pepper and salt

What you need

Toaster

Fork

Garlic press

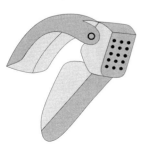

Knife

Teaspoon

Bowl

Scissors

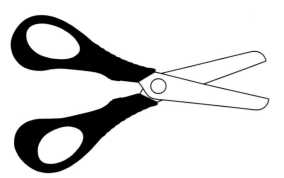

Ask an adult to prepare the oven

What to do

1 In a bowl add:
   2 tsp. butter

3 leaves parsley

1 tsp. olive oil

Pinch of salt and pepper

1 clove crushed garlic

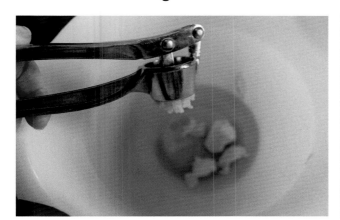

2 Mix with a fork

3 Toast the bread.

4 Spread on mixture.

5 Ask an adult to put in the oven for 5–10 minutes at 180°C.

Banana, strawberry and yoghurt smoothie

Ingredients

2 bananas

3 tbsp. yoghurt

10 strawberries

What you need

Colander

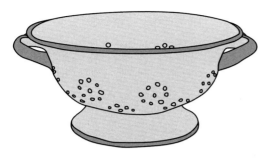

Knife

Tablespoon

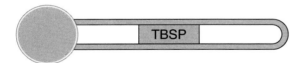

Chopping board

Blender

What to do

1 Wash and cut the strawberries.

2   Peel and slice banana.

3   Add 3 tbs. yoghurt.

4   Ask an adult to blend.

5   Pour into a cup to serve.

Vegetable soup

Ingredients

Vegetables

Stock cube

Water

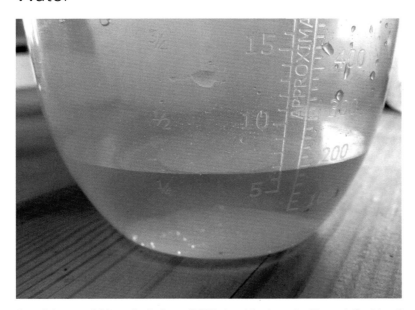

What you need

Colander

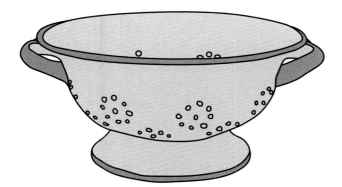

Peeler

Chopping board

Knife

Jug

Soup maker

What to do

1 Select and wash your vegetables.

2 Prepare your vegetables by peeling, chopping/slicing or tearing them.

3 Place all ingredients in the soup maker.

4 Add one stock cube.

5 Pour water until it reaches the minimum line.

6 Ask an adult to put in the soup maker.

Cake

Ingredients

Eggs
Butter
Sugar
Flour

Bowl

Balance scales

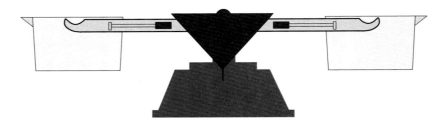

Small spoon

Wooden spoon

Cake tin

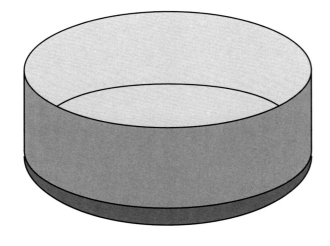

Remember to ask an adult to turn the oven on.

What to do

1 Balance eggs with flour.

2 Put flour in the bowl.

3 Balance eggs with sugar.

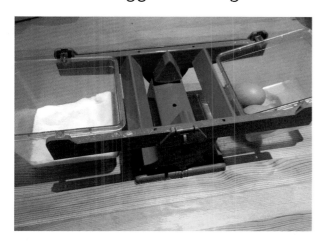

4 Put sugar in the bowl.

5 Balance eggs with butter.

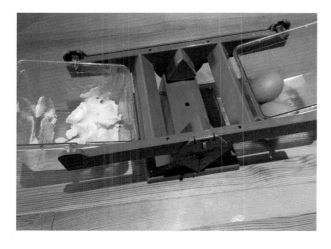

6 Put butter in the bowl.

7 Crack the eggs.

8 Mix.

9 Grease tin.

10 Pour into tin.

11 Ask an adult to put in the oven for 15 minutes at 180°C.

Biscuits

Ingredients

Flour
Sugar
Butter
An egg
Vanilla extract

What you need

Bowl

Tablespoon

Teaspoon

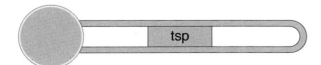

Rolling pin

Wooden spoon

Baking tray

Cutters

What to do

1 Count 8 tbsp. of sugar into a bowl.

2 Count 8 tbsp. of butter into the bowl.

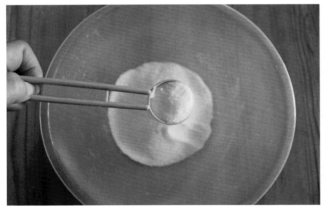

3 Mix.

4 Crack 1 egg into the bowl.

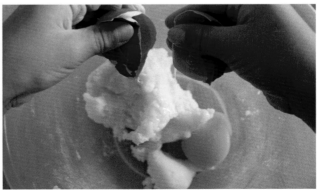

5 Add 2 tsp. of vanilla extract.

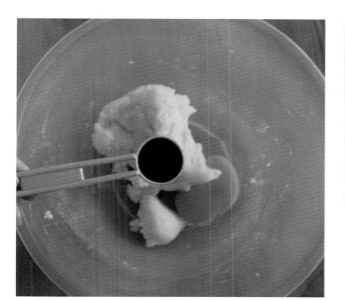

6 Add 25 tbsp. of flour.

7 Mix and then knead into a dough.

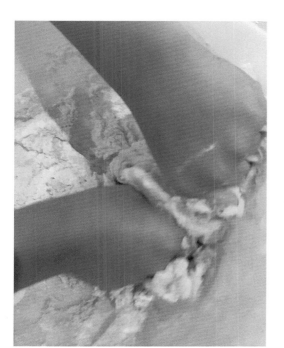

8 Roll out dough.

9 Grease baking tray with butter.

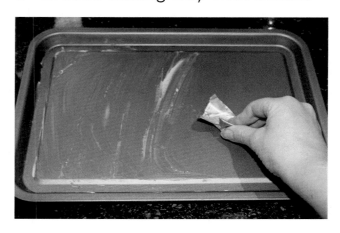

10 Cut shapes and put on the baking tray.

11 Ask an adult to bake for 10 minutes at 180°C.

Bread

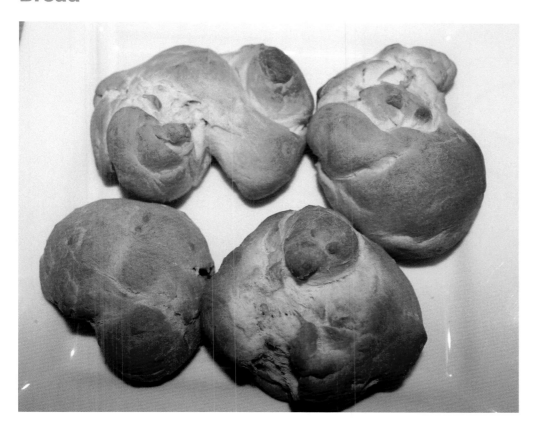

Ingredients

Strong flour
Salt
Yeast
Oil
Warm water

187

What you need

Bowl

Teaspoon

tsp

Measuring cup

Wooden spoon

Baking tray

Jug

Oven

Remember to ask an adult to turn the oven on.

What to do

1 Put 3 cups flour in the bowl.

2 Put 1 tsp. salt in the bowl.

3 Put 2 tsp. yeast in the bowl.

4 Make a well in the middle.

5 Add 9 tsp. oil in the well.

6 Add water. Measure to the line (170 ml).

7 Mix.

8 Sprinkle flour on the table.

9 Knead for 10 minutes.

10 Leave in the bowl for 1 hour.

11 Shape and put on tray.

12 Ask an adult to put in the oven for 15 minutes at 190°C.

KS1 recipes

Sandwiches/wraps

1 Choose your base.

2 Select and prepare your filling.

3 Fill your wrap or sandwich. You could use butter or leave plain.

4 Put your wrap or sandwich together.

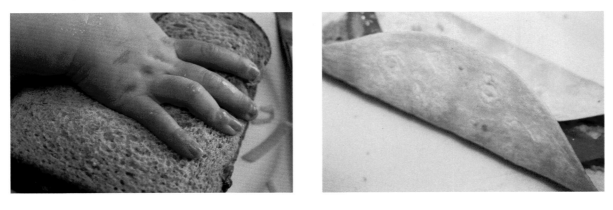

5 Cut into ½ or ¼.

Vegetable tarts

Ingredients

Puff pastry
Vegetables for roasting e.g. red onion, courgette, pepper or tomato
Olive oil
Optional: feta cheese

What you need

Colander

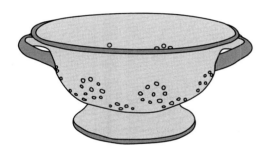

Chopping board

Rolling pin

Baking tray

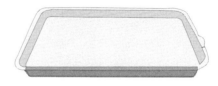

Knife

Remember to ask an adult to turn the oven on.

What to do

1 Wash and cut the vegetables.

2 Drizzle on a little olive oil and ask an adult to roast the vegetables for 15 minutes at 200°C.

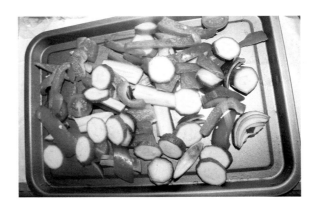

3 Spread vegetables on rolled out puff pastry (add crumbled feta here if wanted).

4 Curl up the edges and ask an adult to return to the oven for 12–15 minutes at 200°C.

Smoothies

Ingredients

Fruit and vegetables
Juice or water

What you need

Colander

Chopping board

Knife

Blender

What to do

1 Wash fruit and vegetables.

2 Prepare fruit and vegetables.

3 Add to the container, adding
water or juice to the fill line.

4 Ask an adult to blend.

5 Pour into a cup to serve.

Leek and potato soup

Ingredients

2 leeks
3 potatoes
Crème fraiche
Stock cube
Garlic

What you need

Peeler

Chopping board

Knife

Soup maker

Colander

Garlic press

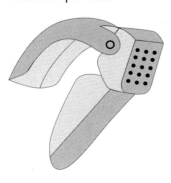

1   Peel and chop potatoes.

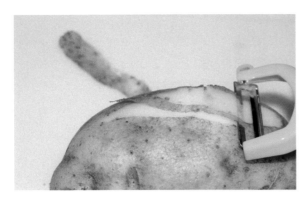

2   Wash, prepare and slice the leek.

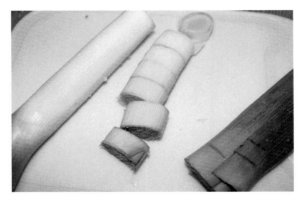

3   Peel and press the garlic.

4   Place all ingredients in the soup maker.

5 Add one stock cube and ½ pot crème fraiche.

6 Pour water until it reaches the minimum line.

7 Ask an adult to turn the soup maker on.

Banana loaf

Ingredients

100 g caster sugar
100 g self-raising flour
2 mashed bananas
1 tsp. baking powder
2 tsp. milk
1 egg
50 g butter

What you need

Bowl

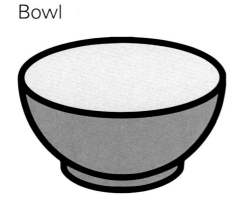

Teaspoon

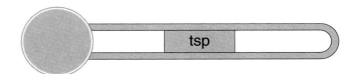

Small spoon

Fork

Scales

Loaf tin

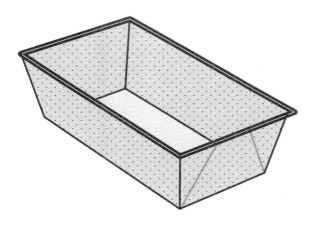

Baking paper

Remember to ask an adult to turn the oven on.

Wooden spoon

What to do

1   Mix all the ingredients in the bowl (make sure you have mashed the banana first). Make sure you mix it very well.

2   Grease loaf tin and line with baking paper.

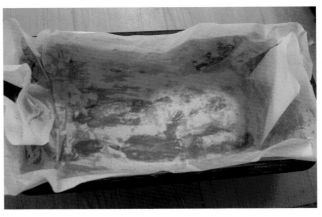

3   Spoon mixture into loaf tin.

4   Ask an adult to bake in the oven for 30 minutes at 160°C.

Carrot cake

Ingredients

Self-raising flour
1 egg
Brown sugar
Oil
Raisins
Carrots

What you need

Bowl

Scales

Peeler

Grater

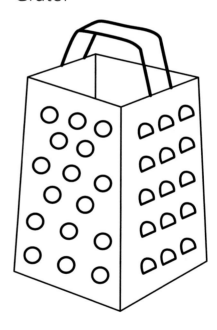

Tablespoon

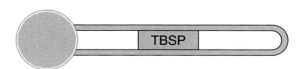

Wooden spoon

Muffin tray

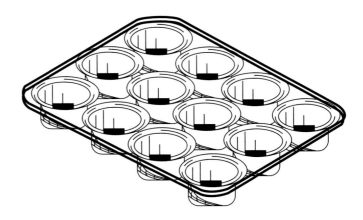

Oven

Cake cases

What to do

1 Put 100 g brown sugar in a bowl.

2 Crack an egg into the bowl.

3 Add 100 g self-raising flour.

4 Peel and grate 100 g carrots and add to the mixture.

5 Add 50 g raisins.

6 Add 5 tbsp. oil.

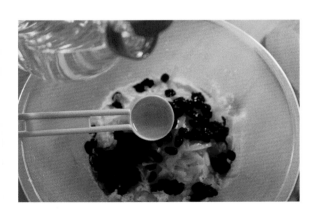

7 Mix together well.

8 Spread the mixture evenly into cases and tin.

9 Ask an adult to bake for 15 minutes at 180°C.

Flapjacks

Ingredients

50 g porridge
125 g melted butter
2 tbsp. honey

Optional

Raisins
Dried berries
Desiccated coconut
What else could you try?

What you need

Bowl

Small spoon

Scales

Small tin

Wooden spoon

Tablespoon

Remember to ask an adult to turn the oven on.

What to do

1 Mix all the ingredients in the bowl.

2 Grease the tin with butter.

3 Press the mixture into the tin.

4 Ask an adult to put in the oven for 35 minutes at 150°C.

Fruit crumble

Ingredients

150 g plain flour
100 g cubed butter
120 g brown sugar
Fruit
Cinnamon (optional)

What you need

Bowl

Scales

Chopping board

Peeler

Knife

Oven dish

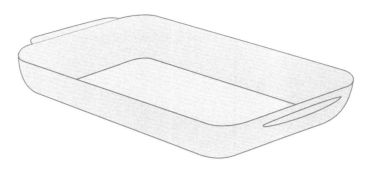

Wooden spoon

Oven

What to do

1 Put flour, butter and 90 g sugar into a bowl.

2 Rub in butter until mixture becomes breadcrumbs.

3 Peel and chop your chosen fruit.

4 Place fruit in an ovenproof dish. Sprinkle 30 g brown sugar then add crumble mix. You may add 1 tsp. cinnamon if you like.

5 Add crumble mix on top.

6 Ask an adult to put in the oven for 45 minutes or until brown at 180°C.

Gingerbread

Ingredients

250 g flour
1 tbsp. baking powder
1 tbsp. ginger
100 g butter
140 g sugar
1 egg
1 tbsp. golden syrup
Decoration if desired

What you need

Bowl

Rolling pin

Baking tray

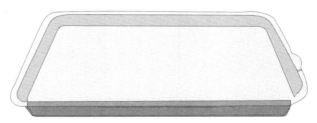

Scales

Oven

Tablespoon

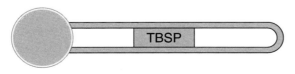

What to do

1   Put 250 g flour into a bowl.

2   Add 1 tbsp. of baking powder.

3   Add 1 tbsp. of ginger.

4   Add 100 g of butter.

5   Rub in butter.

6   Add 140 g sugar.

7 Add 3 tbsp. of syrup.

8 Add 1 egg.

9 Mix.

10 Knead into a dough.

11 Roll out dough.

12 Cut out shapes.

13 Place onto a baking tray.

14 Ask an adult to bake for 15 minutes at 180°C.

15 Decorate as you like.

Bread

Ingredients

360 g strong flour
1 tsp. salt
2 tsp. yeast
3 tbsp. oil
170 ml warm water

Optional extras:

Herbs
Seeds
Olives
Sun-dried tomatoes

Please note: You can choose to use wholemeal or white strong flour

What you need

Tablespoon

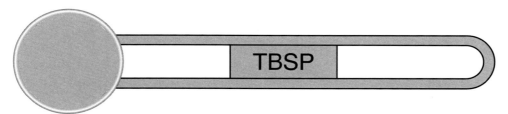

Teaspoon

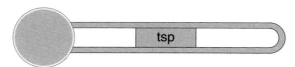

Bowl

Jug

Oven

Baking tray

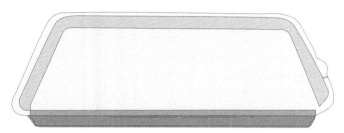

What to do

1 Put the flour in a mixing bowl.
2 Add the salt and yeast to the flour and mix.
3 Make a well in the middle of the mixture.
4 Pour oil in the middle of the mixture.
5 Pour warm water in the middle.
6 Mix together.
7 Sprinkle a generous portion of flour on the table.
8 Knead the dough for 10 minutes.
9 Leave in a bowl for approximately 1 hour to rise. The warmer the place, the more quickly the dough will rise.
10 Consider if you would like to add any other ingredients to your dough. You can add these ingredients after the bread has risen.
11 Shape your bread and place onto baking paper on a baking tray. Will you make one large loaf to share or make small rolls? What shape will you make?
12 Ask an adult to put the bread in the oven for 15 minutes at 190°C.

Muffins

Ingredients

225 g mashed bananas
1 egg
125 ml water
125 ml vegetable oil
250 g wholemeal flour
1 tsp. bicarbonate of soda
2¼ tsp. baking powder
A good portion of fruit/
vegetables e.g. blueberries,
raspberries, raisins, grated
carrot or grated courgette

What you need

Large bowl

Knife

Wooden spoon

Muffin tray

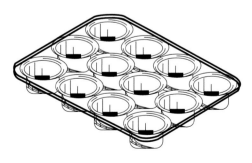

Fork

Jug

Teaspoon

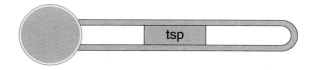

tsp

Metal spoon

Muffin cases

Oven

Possibly: grater or peeler

What to do

1 Mix all the ingredients in the bowl apart from the fruit or vegetables.

2 Cut, chop or grate the fruit or vegetables. Fold into the mixture.

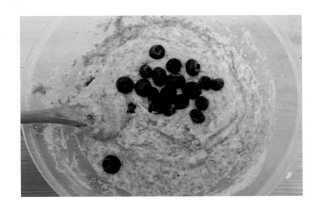

3 Spoon into cases.

4 Ask an adult to bake in the oven for 25 minutes at 180°C.

Scones

Ingredients

350 g self-raising flour
Pinch of salt
1 tbsp. baking powder
85 g butter cut into cubes
3 tbsp. caster sugar
175 ml milk
Extra ingredients such as
cheese, fruit, raisins

What you need

Bowl

Rolling pin

Baking tray

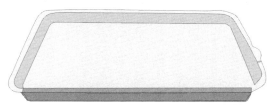

Knife

Circular cutters

Jug

Oven

Brush

Spoon

Possibly: grater

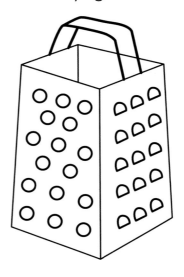

What to do

1 Mix the flour, salt and baking powder in a bowl.
2 Add butter and rub until the mixture looks like fine breadcrumbs.

3 Stir in the sugar.
4 Add any extras you would like e.g. blueberries, raisins, grated cheese, chopped dried or fresh fruit.

5 Stir in milk.
6 Knead with your hands into a stiff dough.

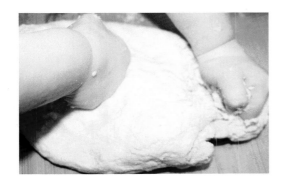

7 Roll out dough until it is 2 cm thick.
8 Grease baking tray with butter.
9 Cut out circles and brush them with milk. Place on a baking tray.

10 Ask an adult to put in the oven for 12–15 minutes at 220°C.

Cheese straws

Ingredients

150 g butter
75 g grated cheese
225 g plain flour
½ tsp. mustard powder
1 tbsp. water

What you need

Baking tray

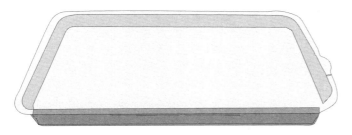

Bowl

Knife

Scales

Teaspoon

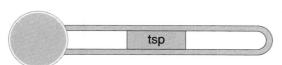

Tablespoon

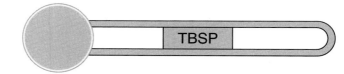

Rolling pin

Oven

What to do

1 Grease a baking tray with butter.

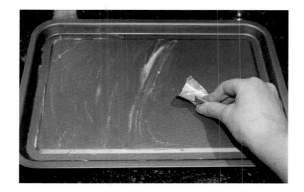

2 Cut the butter into small cubes and place into a bowl.

3 Add flour and mix together until the mixture resembles breadcrumbs.

4 Add 60 g cheese, the mustard powder and 1 tbsp. water. Mix into dough.

5 Roll onto a floured surface. Roll until 1 cm thick.

6 Cut into 1 cm strips.

7 Shape your straws.

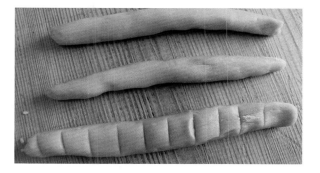

Rolls

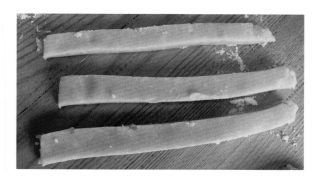

Twists

Strips

Add seeds using egg whites for glue!

8 Place on a baking tray and sprinkle with the remaining cheese.

9 Ask an adult to put into an oven for 15 minutes at 190°C.

Hot cross buns

Ingredients

500 g flour
½ tsp. salt
2 tsp. mixed spice
50 g caster sugar
50 g butter, chopped into cubes
200 g mixed dried fruit
1 packet dried yeast
200 ml milk
2 eggs
Flour for crosses

What you need

2 bowls

Scales

Knife

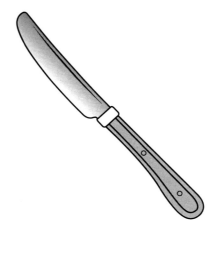

Baking tray

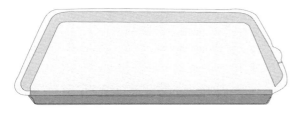

Baking tray

Whisk

Baking paper

Measuring jug

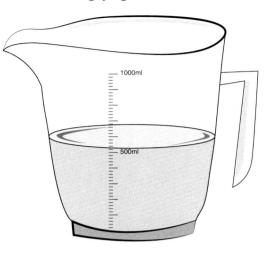

1000ml

500ml

Teaspoon

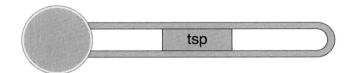

tsp

Spoon

What to do

1 Tip the flour into the bowl and stir in the salt, sugar and mixed spice.
2 Rub in the butter.
3 Stir in yeast.
4 Beat milk and eggs together in another bowl.
5 Combine the two bowls together.
6 Add mixed dried fruit and stir with a knife until this is a moist dough.
7 Leave to soak for 5 minutes.
8 Shape into 8 buns and put on baking sheet.

  9 Leave for 30 minutes until they have risen half in size again.
10 Ask an adult to heat the oven to 200°C.
11 Mix 2 tsp. water with 3 tsp. flour, making a paste.
12 Roll out into strips and place on top of buns.

13 Ask an adult to bake for 12–15 minutes at 200°C.

Pancakes

1 Put 100 g flour in a bowl.
2 Add 2 eggs.
3 Add 300 ml of milk.
4 Whisk the ingredients together.
5 Ask an adult to fry the pancake.
6 Choose your toppings.
7 Fill and roll your pancake.

Falafel burgers or balls

Ingredients

400g can chickpeas
1 tsp. chilli powder
1 tsp. ground cumin
1 tsp. ground coriander
2 tbsp. plain flour
1 garlic clove
1 small red onion
Olive oil (for cooking)

What you need

Colander

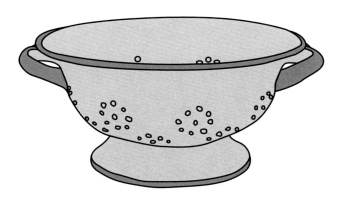

Mortar and pestle

Chopping board

Knife

Garlic press

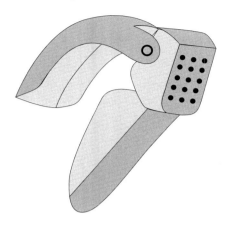

Tablespoon

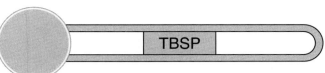

Teaspoon

Frying pan

Bowl

Hob (use with an adult)

1   Drain chickpeas well and crush in mortar
and pestle.

2   Chop the onion as small as
you can.

3   Put the crushed chickpeas, onion,
all the spices and the flour into a
large bowl.

4 Add crushed garlic, a pinch of
   salt and mix extremely well.

5 Shape into 4 burgers or 8
   balls.

6 Ask an adult to fry the burgers
   or balls in a little olive oil for 5
   minutes on either side.

Quiche

Pastry ingredients

175 g flour
75 g butter
Water

Filling ingredients

150 g grated cheese
200 ml milk or cream
4 eggs
Vegetables

What you need

Quiche dish / tray

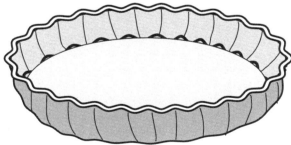

Grater

Bowl

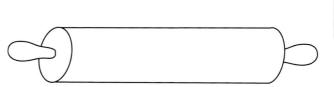

Oven

Rolling pin

Wooden spoon

Baking beans

Scissors

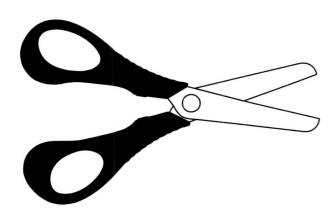

Cutters

Jug

Knife

Chopping board

Scales

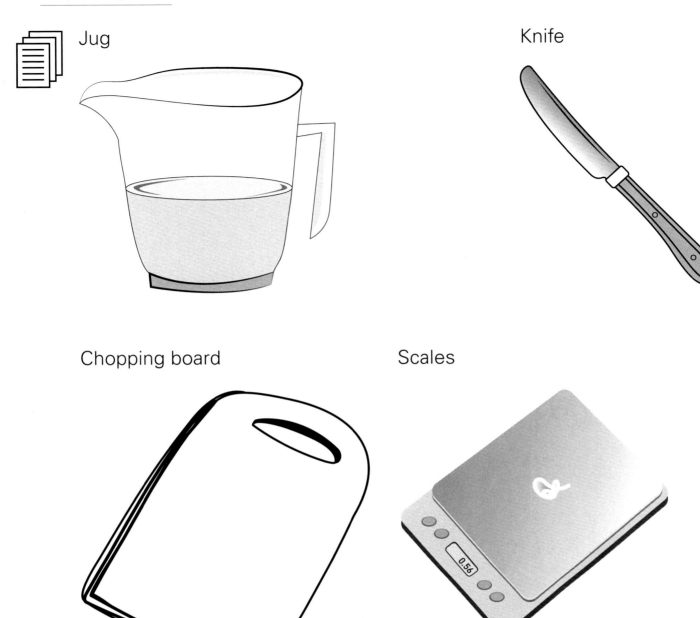

What to do

1 (To make the pastry) Rub the butter and flour together.

2 Add a little water and knead until it makes a firm dough. Then leave the dough to rest for half an hour in the fridge.

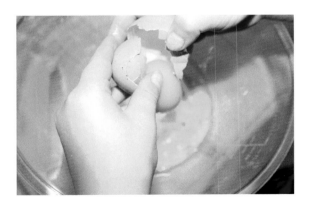

3 (To make the filling) Crack the eggs into the bowl.

4 Add the grated cheese and milk.

5 Chop or cut the vegetables you would like to add.

6 Add these to the filling and mix.

7 Grease the dish or tray with a little butter.

8 Take the dough out of the fridge and roll the pastry.

9 Cut the pastry to size and fit it into the tray or dish.

10 Place greaseproof paper and then baking beans on the pastry and ask an adult to bake for 15 minutes at 200°C. Then remove the beans and bake for five more minutes.

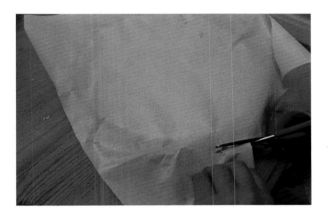

11 Pour the filling into the pastry and bake in the oven for 15 minutes at 200°C or until golden brown.

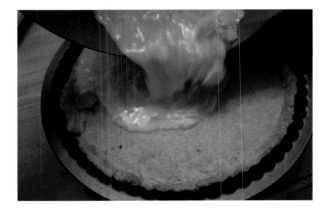

Pizza

Ingredients for base

300 g strong flour
1 tsp. yeast
1 tsp. salt
1 tsp. olive oil
200 ml warm water

What you need

Large bowl

Jug

Wooden spoon

Tea towel

Scales

What to do for base

1 Put flour in the bowl with yeast and salt and stir.

2 Make a well and stir in water and olive oil. Softly stir with spoon until the mixture is a soft dough.

3 Knead on a floured surface for 5 minutes.

4 Leave under a tea towel to rise.

Ingredients for topping

Passata
Cheese of your choice
Vegetables of choice
Basil/olive oil (optional)

What you need for topping

Spoon

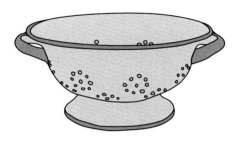

Colander

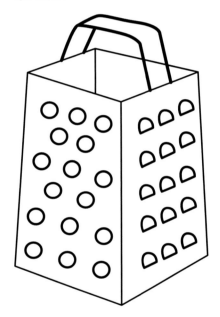

Grater

Oven

Chopping board

Knife

Rolling pin

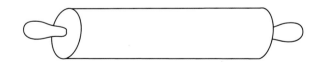

Copyright material from Suzie Strutt (2019), *Inspiring Learning Through Cooking*, Routledge

What to do for topping

1 Share out the dough.
2 Roll out the dough on a floured surface, shaping the pizzas.
3 Spread passata on the base.
4 Grate cheese on top.
5 Wash, chop and add vegetables of your choice.
6 Ask an adult to cook in the oven at 220°C for 6–10 minutes.
7 Add olive oil or basil if required.

Jam or lemon tarts

Ingredients for pastry

250 g plain flour
100 g butter cut into cubes
2 or 3 tbsp. water
Salt

Ingredients for filling

Jam or lemon curd

What you need

Muffin tray

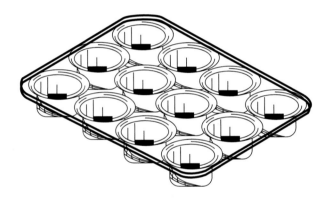

Knife

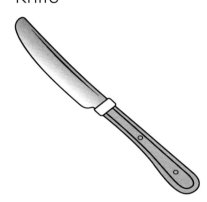

Rolling pin

Small spoon

Cutters

Cling film

Bowl

What to do

1 Put flour, butter and a pinch of salt into a bowl.
2 Rub into breadcrumbs using fingertips.

3 Add 2 or 3 tbsp. of water and stir with a cold knife.
4 Mould into a ball of dough.

5 Wrap in cling film and chill for 30 minutes.
6 After 30 minutes sprinkle flour on the surface.

7 Roll out pastry.
8 Cut out shapes.

9 Press into tin.
10 Spoon in jam or lemon curd.

11 Assemble the tops of the tarts.
12 Ask an adult to cook in the oven for 15 minutes at 180°C.

Book of dips

Chop carrots, celery and pepper to eat with these delicious dips.

Hummus

1 Pour ¾ of the liquid out of the can of chickpeas.
2 Crush the chickpeas in a mortar and pestle.
3 Add 1½ tbsp. of tahini paste.
4 Squeeze the juice of ½ lemon.
5 Add 2 tbsp. of olive oil.
6 Add 2 cloves crushed garlic.
7 Mix.

Guacamole

1 Peel one avocado.
2 Mash with a fork.
3 Squeeze in some lime or lemon.

Tomato salsa

1 Chop tomatoes.
2 Crush garlic.
3 Mix.

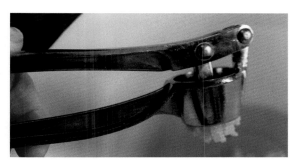

Optional: add a little olive oil

Cucumber and mint raita

1 Grate cucumber and squeeze out excess water.
2 Add natural yoghurt.
3 Add chopped mint.

Feta and spinach

1 Chop and crush feta.
2 Tear spinach and crush.
3 Mix.

Risk/benefit assessment for cooking in EYFS

Benefits

PSE	Children will have the opportunity to: • Negotiate with peers • Develop independence and confidence • Work co-operatively	CL	Children will have the opportunity to: • Follow instructions of more than two parts • Use talk to organise, sequence and clarify thinking • Develop vocabulary
PD	Children will have the opportunity to: • Use tools with increasing control • Develop strength in wrist and control in fine and gross motor skills by mixing, kneading and rolling, whisking, rolling, pouring, stirring, moulding, shaping etc.	PD	Children will have the opportunity to: • Show some understanding that good practices with regard to exercise, eating, sleeping and hygiene can contribute to good health • Show understanding of the need for safety when tackling new challenges, and consider and manage some risks • Show understanding of how to transport and store equipment safely • Practice some appropriate safety measures without direct supervision • Explore raw ingredients and their properties • Develop their understanding of healthy foods
L	Children will have the opportunity to: • Recognise familiar words • Know information is relayed in the form of print • Know that print carries meaning • Read and understand simple sentences • Use phonic knowledge to decode familiar words and also read some uncommon words • Demonstrate understanding when talking to others about what they have read	M Number	Children will have the opportunity to: • Count reliably to 20 • Solve problems involving halving and sharing • Compare, describe and solve practical problems for weight • Use the language of weight • Order two items by weight • Explore shape, capacity and time • Create and explore patterns
UW	Children will have the opportunity to: • Talk about and observe changes through cooling, cooking, freezing, raising • Explore the properties of raw ingredients • Consider traditional and cultural recipes • Know how to operate simple equipment • Select and use equipment for particular purposes	EAD	Children will have the opportunity to: • Realise that tools are used for a purpose • Use simple tools and techniques competently and appropriately • Represent their own ideas

Risks and actions

Establishment:		Assessed by:		Date:	
Hazard/Risk	**Who is at Risk**	**Control Measures**			**Risk Rating**
Sharp equipment Cuts	Staff, pupils, volunteer helpers	• Considered choice of appropriate knives (safety knives) • Controlled storage and use of sharp knives • Pupils taught correct techniques for use of knives • Sharp knives to be washed separately and not left in the sink			Low
Slippery floors Slips and trips	Staff, pupils, volunteer helpers	• Floors cleaned regularly • Spillages to be cleaned immediately • Paper towels to be used on small areas of spilt water			Low
Use of cookers, microwaves, soup maker, blender, toasters Electric shock, fire, explosion	Staff, pupils, volunteer helpers	• Food to cooked by staff only using the oven/hob in the kitchen • Soup maker and blender to only be used by adults and only plugged in out of reach of children • Electrical equipment is subject to regular safety inspection and testing (PAT) • Children to be supervised at all times when using or observing, microwave, the toaster • The oven will not be used for any purposes other than cooking • The oven is sited away from flammable materials, doorways, passageways and fire escape routes • When the hob is being used the oven will be away from wall displays			Low
Food poisoning	Staff, pupils, volunteer helpers	• Pupils taught the need for personal hygiene • Staff and all adults to wash hands before handling food and after using the toilet • Water, soap and disposable towels always available • Cuts and scrapes covered with waterproof adhesive dressings • Long hair tied back • Foods to be stored in the classroom in suitable containers to protect from contamination • Butter and dairy products to be kept in the school fridges over night • 'Use by' and 'best before' dates should be checked • Food appropriately covered/wrapped for children to take home • All equipment is stored in secure, clean conditions and used only for food preparation • All preparation done on the designated cooking table. Work surfaces cleaned with a multi-purpose cleaner prior to food preparation • Any other classroom tables need to be used will be covered with a clean plastic sheet • Adequate rubbish bins for waste food which are emptied daily			Low
Pupils with food allergies	Pupils	• All staff/volunteers made aware of pupils with allergies or sensitivities to food. A list including photographs of children is kept on display inside the teacher's cupboard for all staff to check • All staff/volunteers made aware of ingredients in foodstuffs • Tables cleaned before any food preparation • Alternative ingredients used for pupils with allergies, e.g. dairy free butter • Equipment cleaned thoroughly after each use to prevent cross-contamination			Low

Risk/benefit assessment for cooking in KS1

Benefits

Building upon social skills and working collaboratively
Problem solving
Co-operation and decision-making skills
Building upon communication and language skills
Exploring food choices and healthy eating
Using tools, developing fine and gross motor skills
Considering and assessing own safety risks
Consolidate and embed taught skills in Literacy and Mathematics in a real-life context
Demonstrate and apply good hygiene procedures
Cross curricular learning, covering a broad range of subjects
DT curriculum

Risks and actions

Establishment:		Assessed by:		Date:	
Hazard/Risk	**Who Is At risk**	**Control Measures**			**Risk Rating**
Sharp equipment Cuts	Staff, pupils, volunteer helpers	• Considered choice of appropriate knives (safety knives) • Controlled storage and use of sharp knives • Pupils taught correct techniques for use of knives • Sharp knives to be washed separately and not left in the sink			Low
Slippery floors Slips and trips	Staff, pupils, volunteer helpers	• Floors cleaned regularly • Spillages to be cleaned immediately • Paper towels to be used on small areas of spilt water			Low
Use of cookers, microwaves, soup maker, blender, toasters Electric shock, fire, explosion	Staff, pupils, volunteer helpers	• Food to cooked by staff only using the oven/hob in the kitchen • Soup maker and blender to only be used by adults and only plugged in out of reach of children • Electrical equipment is subject to regular safety inspection and testing (PAT) • Children to be supervised at all times when using or observing, microwave, the toaster • The oven will not be used for any purposes other than cooking • The oven is sited away from flammable materials, doorways, passageways and fire escape routes • When the hob is being used the oven will be away from wall displays			Low
Food poisoning	Staff, pupils, volunteer helpers	• Pupils taught the need for personal hygiene • Staff and all adults to wash hands before handling food and after using the toilet • Water, soap and disposable towels always available • Cuts and scrapes covered with waterproof adhesive dressings • Long hair tied back • Foods to be stored in the classroom in suitable containers to protect from contamination • Butter and dairy products to be kept in the school fridges over night • 'Use by' and 'best before' dates should be checked • Food appropriately covered/wrapped for children to take home • All equipment is stored in secure, clean conditions and used only for food preparation • All preparation done on the designated cooking table. Work surfaces cleaned with a multi-purpose cleaner prior to food preparation • Any other classroom tables need to be used will be covered with a clean plastic sheet • Adequate rubbish bins for waste food which are emptied daily			Low
Pupils with food allergies	Pupils	• All staff/volunteers made aware of pupils with allergies or sensitivities to food. A list including photographs of children is kept on display inside the teacher's cupboard for all staff to check • All staff/volunteers made aware of ingredients in foodstuffs • Tables cleaned before any food preparation • Alternative ingredients used for pupils with allergies, e.g. dairy free butter • Equipment cleaned thoroughly after each use to prevent cross contamination			Low

Index